PRO[...]

It's been making headlines and front-page news nationwide.

It's prescribed hundreds of thousands of times every month.

It rescues millions from conditions as diverse as depression, anxiety, and eating disorders.

Is Prozac a wonder drug that effectively relieves depression while causing only minimal side effects?

Or is it a dangerous weapon that can spark agitation, violence—even suicide?

Here is the first guide that separates the facts from the myths about Prozac—from the publishers of *The Pill Book*.

A PILL BOOK GUIDE

Everything You Need to Know About
PROZAC

Other Bantam Books

THE PILL BOOK, 4th revised edition, Harold Silverman
  and Gilbert Simon
THE PILL BOOK GUIDE TO SAFE DRUG USE, Harold
  Silverman
THE PILL BOOK GUIDE TO CHILDREN'S
  MEDICATIONS, Michael Mitchell, M.D.
BANTAM MEDICAL DICTIONARY, revised edition

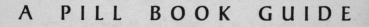

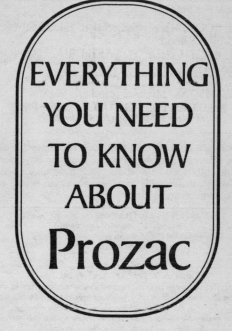

EVERYTHING YOU NEED TO KNOW ABOUT Prozac

JEFFREY M. JONAS, M.D.

AND

RON SCHAUMBURG

BANTAM BOOKS

NEW YORK · TORONTO · LONDON · SYDNEY · AUCKLAND

The authors wish to thank Dan Montopoli, Larry Chilnick, Toni Burbank, and Bob Oskam for making this book possible.

Special thanks to Sandra Choron.

We are grateful to our wives, Shelley Jonas and Susan Schaumburg, for their love and support.

EVERYTHING YOU NEED TO KNOW ABOUT PROZAC
A Bantam Nonfiction Book / May 1991

The information contained in this book is intended to comple-ment, not substitute for, the advice of your own physician, with whom you should consult about your individual needs. You should always consult with your own physician before starting any medical treatment or diet.

*BANTAM NONFICTION and the portrayal of a
boxed "b" are trademarks of
Bantam Books, a division of Bantam Doubleday
Dell Publishing Group, Inc.*

All rights reserved.
Copyright © 1991 by March Tenth, Inc.
*No part of this book may be reproduced or transmitted in any
form or by any means, electronic or mechanical, including
photocopying, recording, or by any information storage and
retrieval system, without permission in writing from the publisher.
For information address: Bantam Books.*

*Designed by Stanley S. Drate, Folio Graphics Co., Inc.
Packaged by Rapid Transcript, a division
of March Tenth, Inc.*

ISBN 0-553-29192-0

Published simultaneously in the United States and Canada

---

*Bantam Books are published by Bantam Books, a division of Bantam Doubleday
Dell Publishing Group, Inc. Its trademark, consisting of the words "Bantam
Books" and the portrayal of a rooster, is Registered in U.S. Patent and Trademark
Office and in other countries. Marca Registrada. Bantam Books, 666 Fifth
Avenue, New York, New York 10103.*

PRINTED IN THE UNITED STATES OF AMERICA

OPM   0 9 8 7 6 5 4 3 2 1

CONTENTS

INTRODUCTION

Melissa* entered my office, her face as sunny as the burgeoning spring visible through the window. The contrast from the Melissa I remembered from the month before was astounding. For a minute I thought I was seeing another person. And in a way, I was.

When I had admitted her to the hospital a month before, this thirty-three-year-old housewife felt as low as she had ever felt in her life. She wanted to cry but couldn't. She had no energy, took no pleasure in anything, and was barely able to run the household and look after her nine-month-old daughter. She fought constantly with her husband and was sure he was about to leave her. She felt horribly guilty that she was destroying her family, and could see no hope that things would ever change. The future, she said, was like a long black tunnel, with no light at the end, with no way out.

Her family doctor had given her a prescription for an antidepressant, which she had taken faithfully, but

---

*All patient names and identifying details have been changed to protect privacy. Some patient anecdotes are composites drawn from a number of actual case records.

which made no difference. The situation had deteriorated by the time she came to me. I admitted her to the hospital and switched her medication.

A month later, almost completely recovered, she was on her way home and had stopped by my office to say good-bye. "I feel like a veil has been lifted from my brain," she said, smiling. "It was as if I'd had a headache every day for a year, and now it's gone."

The thing that made all the difference was a new drug: Prozac.

Two weeks later, however, I got a frantic phone call. It was Melissa. She was crying so much I could hardly make out what she was saying. At first I thought she was suffering a relapse, that her medication had quit working and her depression was back. It turned out she had heard someone on the news reporting that Prozac could cause people to become hostile, violent, even suicidal. "I feel so good with this drug," she sobbed. "Is it going to make me kill myself? Are you going to take it away from me?"

PROZAC IN THE NEWS

In the spring of 1990 *Newsweek* magazine featured Prozac on its cover. The illustration featured an enormous two-toned drug capsule floating dreamily above a serene and endless landscape. The words on the cover trumpeted, "PROZAC: A Breakthrough Drug for Depression." Titled "The Promise of Prozac," the article included pictures of happy, smiling people whose lives had changed after taking Prozac. Without reading a word of the article you could pretty much guess its tone: Clap your hands, ring the bells, another medical miracle!

Just a few months earlier, *New York* magazine had run a similar piece, also as a cover story, titled "Bye-Bye Blues: A New Wonder Drug for Depression." This article also contained lots of uplifting anecdotes about patients whose lives had been turned around after using Prozac.

Seizing on reports that Prozac, unlike other antidepressants, did not usually promote weight gain, the *National Enquirer*, in bold headlines, called Prozac a "miracle diet pill." TV talk shows buzzed with Prozac prattle. Stories touted Prozac as a treatment for everything from eating disorders to personality disorders, from obesity to substance abuse. One psychiatrist, quoted in the *New York* article, even wondered if one day *everybody* might be taking Prozac.

A Happy Pill that ends all of your problems and has no serious side effects? *And that may even help you lose weight*? Who wouldn't want such a thing? Due largely to such media exposure, people with only a vague idea of what depression was decided they were depressed, visited their doctors, and demanded a prescription for Prozac. Sales of the drug—already the best-selling antidepressant on the market, even at a hefty sticker price of around a dollar and a half for each 20-milligram capsule—continued to skyrocket. Over 800,000 prescriptions for Prozac were being written each month.

There were some clouds on the horizon, however, threatening to rain on this media parade. Somewhere toward the end of the *Newsweek* article, there was mention of a report from Harvard Medical School. That report, which appeared in the February 1990 issue of the *American Journal of Psychiatry*, was—on the surface, anyway—alarming. It warned that *as many as 7.5 percent of patients taking Prozac may be at risk of experiencing "intense, violent suicidal preoccupation."*

Then other reports began trickling in of people who were being treated with Prozac for depression and became hostile or violent. Some of these people lashed out violently, attempting suicide or performing acts of self-mutilation. In one notorious case, a man went on a rampage, killing eight people, wounding a dozen others, then killing himself. An autopsy revealed the presence of Prozac in his bloodstream.

Product liability lawyers saw their opportunity. Eli

Lilly, Prozac's manufacturer, was peppered with lawsuits charging that the drug caused some people to become suicidal or, even worse, triggered violent rampages. The suits—most of which cited the Harvard study as their supporting evidence—claimed that Lilly had not tested the drug sufficiently before putting it on the market.

The fire was fanned again when, in the fall of 1990, someone shot and killed Rabbi Meir Kahane, the controversial founder of the Jewish Defense League. Officials subsequently revealed that the accused gunman was a psychiatric patient being treated with Prozac. However, the suspect was also taking as many as *four other psychiatric medications*. He had suffered a severe electrical shock during an industrial accident some years earlier, losing partial use of one of his legs. Though highly qualified as an engineer, he could only find jobs as a maintenance worker. Despite these circumstances, any one of which might have been enough to trigger violence in someone suffering from severe mental illness, the implication in news reports was that Prozac was to blame for what had happened.

THE "BORING" MEDICINE

Media attention suggests that Prozac is an "exciting" medicine. Frankly, I think it's boring. Why? Because by and large it works—it works well and there are very few surprises.

Not that this is to be viewed as a complaint. In medicine, "boring" is better. Doctors would gladly forego the "excitement" of dealing with side effects, adverse reactions, and emergency phone calls at four in the morning. The excitement for them comes from hearing patients like Melissa tell how their lives have changed— that they feel good for the first time in years, that the "black dog" of depression has stopped nipping at their heels. When treating depression, excitement comes not from something out of the ordinary, but from seeing patients return to normal.

However, with recent reports of people becoming suicidal or violent while taking Prozac, there is a sudden element of concern. "What's this? Prozac—the medical miracle, the breakthrough drug, the promising new star that's supposed to make everyone happy—can drive people to kill themselves?"

THE FACTS OF THE MATTER

News reports do not always tell the whole truth. For one thing, *suicidal thoughts are a known symptom of depression*. According to the psychiatrist's "bible," the *Diagnostic and Statistical Manual of Mental Disorders* (third edition, revised), one of the criteria for recognizing the presence of major depression is

> recurrent thoughts of death (not just fear of dying), recurrent suicidal ideation without a specific plan, or a suicide attempt or a specific plan for committing suicide.

The National Institute of Mental Health (NIMH) has even stated that, for at least 15 percent of severely depressed people, *there is no relief but suicide*. In fact, as many as eight out of ten suicides are believed to be associated with some form of depression. Given that people with depression are known to be at very high risk of suicide, it's extremely hard to prove that suicidality is a result of their medication. After more than two decades of research, it has yet to be proved that a drug therapy *caused* suicidal thinking. The evidence indicates that great numbers of patients *stop* thinking about suicide while on antidepressants.

The lawsuits against Eli Lilly generally claim that the manufacturer failed to test the drug adequately before putting it on the market. In fact, close to 11,000 people had been given Prozac in clinical trials. The United States Food and Drug Administration, which spends years meticulously reviewing the safety data before approving a drug for release, has never issued a warning that Prozac is unsafe. Literally millions of people with depression have taken the drug, and it seems reasonable to infer that Prozac may well have *prevented* thousands of suicides that might otherwise have occurred.

There are many other issues involved here—whether the Harvard study cited reflects good scientific practice; whether a drug can be said to trigger suicide in people suffering from an illness whose symptoms include suicidal tendencies; whether other risk factors for suicide, such as a family history of mental illness, may have some bearing on the problem. This book addresses these and other issues in detail.

You may be wondering, is there in fact any danger associated with Prozac? Of course. Any drug powerful enough to produce a clinical benefit is powerful enough to cause side effects. Usually, as you will see later, the side effects of Prozac—nausea, disturbed sleep, anxiety—are not serious. They go away after a few days, and most people feel so much relief from having their depression lift that they happily tolerate some temporary and minor discomfort.

PROZAC: MIRACLE OR MENACE?

What is happening? Why is a drug that is touted as a "miracle" and a "breakthrough" one day pilloried as a dangerous substance the next? Why can't scientists decide if a chemical substance is good or bad?

This book will help you place these and similar questions in perspective. It will tell you what you need to know about the treatment of depression and other psychiatric disorders that affect millions of people in this country. Effective treatment is available in most cases. Prozac doesn't work for everyone with depression, nor does it work in certain other psychiatric illnesses. It is not by any stretch a "miracle diet pill." But for many people it can indeed be a wonder drug.

This book will help you understand how and when Prozac works—and when and why it doesn't. It will alert you to possible side effects to watch out for. It will examine in some detail the growing controversy about possible suicidal effects, a real concern whenever depression is at issue.

The topics covered in this book include:

- How to recognize the symptoms of depression
- How depression and other illnesses, including bulimia and obsessive-compulsive disorder, may be related
- How chemical chaos in the body and brain can trigger psychiatric illnesses
- How the appropriate use of medications can help correct chemical imbalances
- What Prozac can—and cannot—do
- What alternatives to Prozac are available
- How to read between the lines of a medical report or a scientific study to assess its validity
- How to read between the headlines of a newspaper or magazine to get a clearer picture of reality
- What the future holds for the treatment of depression

The information here will help you become an educated health-care consumer. If you are one of the many struggling to overcome depression or one of the other troubling illnesses discussed in this book, it may help you *and your doctor*, working together, to devise a treatment program to return you to good health.

THE FACES OF DEPRESSION

For ten years a man I'll call Jack had been working with his psychoanalyst to get at the roots of his anguish. He suspected that something terrible had happened to him in his childhood; and he was determined to dig through his psyche, sift through the clues, and piece together his troubled past. He felt that if he could only succeed in this mission, he would finally be free of the feelings of guilt and hopelessness that had dominated his life for so long.

During one session the analyst commented on the fact that this was the tenth anniversary of their first meeting. The analyst meant to reassure Jack about the wonderful progress he had made, but on his way home that afternoon Jack found himself more and more disturbed by that remark. After a decade of digging, he felt he was no closer to the source of his suffering. He decided to try another approach. A friend gave him my telephone number, and a few days later he came to my office.

Jack's decade of suffering had taken its toll. He looked many years older than his actual age of thirty-five. His shoulders were slightly bent; the lines of his face sagged downward, pulled by his own private source of gravity. His voice was noticeably thin, raspy, and flat, as if his lungs lacked the energy to pump enough air.

But it was his eyes, lifeless and dim, that revealed the true depth of his despair.

THE STORY IN YOUR EYES

Depression comes in many varieties. While most depressed people *look* depressed, their faces etched by sadness, their eyes full of pain, some appear agitated and frantic.

Regardless of their social and ethnic backgrounds, despite the different ways their illness affects them, people with depression all bear a strange kind of family resemblance to each other. They all give the appearance of being *trapped* by forces beyond their control. Think about any of the movies or documentaries you've seen that were filmed in prisons. Some of the inmates, beaten down by the system, lie passively on their cots, while others pace the floor, rattling the bars of their cages. Depression produces a kind of emotional prison, with some of its victims unable to leave their beds while others can hardly sit still.

Novelist William Styron chronicled his battle with depression in his book *Darkness Visible: A Memoir of Madness*. In this short but powerful essay he describes depression as resembling "the diabolical discomfort of being imprisoned in a fiercely overheated room." This illness, he writes, is a smothering confinement that produces a "veritable howling tempest in the brain . . .

the gray drizzle of horror induced by depression takes on the quality of physical pain."

Depression causes terrible pain, but not the kind of physical suffering caused by, say, a migraine—that throbbing, jackhammering headache so devastating it can make its victims vomit. The chronic pain of depression is terrible because ultimately it leads to the *absence* of feeling. For people with depression, life is stripped of its pleasures. This loss often shows up as a dullness and emptiness in the eyes. In time depression robs people of their sense of taste, and thus their pleasure in eating. They feel no enjoyment from friends, family, sex. They withdraw farther into their shells, feeling guilty, helpless, and hopeless. As Styron puts it: ". . . because there is no escape from this smothering confinement, it is entirely natural that the victim begins to think ceaselessly of oblivion."

It's hard to explain depression to someone who has never experienced it. Styron calls *depression* a "true wimp of a word" for such a terrible illness. And he's right. To a non-sufferer, "depression" suggests a minor indentation, a slight rut in the road through life. In fact, depression is more like a vast crater from the impact of an emotional meteor.

This book focuses on clinical depression—that is, depression that is serious enough to need treatment. At the other end of the spectrum, feelings of sadness—what some people call the blues—can be an ordinary and appropriate part of everyday living. It *is* depressing when a loved one departs from our lives. For highly sensitive people, the news of the day—homelessness, poverty, cruelty, despair—can be emotionally overwhelming at times. These feelings are largely healthy ones, since they show we are capable of responding emotionally to events and situations; such feelings do not always require treatment. If the depression persists and a person cannot function, however, then action is called for.

THE STATISTICAL FACE OF DEPRESSION

Depression is a surprisingly widespread disorder, often referred to as the "common cold" of psychiatric illness. Depression is the cause of three out of four psychiatric hospitalizations. At any given time 15 percent of adults aged eighteen to seventy-four are significantly depressed. Surprisingly, perhaps as many as three out of every one hundred grade-school children experience major depression. Despite the common perception, the elderly are actually at no greater risk of becoming depressed. The highest rates of the disorder occur among young adults.

Researchers found that the rate of depression among the "baby boomers"—those born between 1945 and 1955—increased markedly, reaching a peak between 1975 and 1980. No one is sure why. Some theories trace the rise to social factors: greater competition for jobs, shifting roles for men and women, a widening gap between expectations and fulfillment, increased drug use, more mobility with less chance to lay down social and familial "roots." There may even have been a change in biological factors that can produce depression, but there is no conclusive evidence to date to prove any of these theories. Interestingly—and fortunately—the rate of depression among people born after 1955 seems to be heading downward.

Studies find that, at some point in their lives, perhaps 12 percent of the men in the United States and up to 26 percent of the women have had or will have an episode of major depression serious enough to require treatment. Some experts put the ratio of depressed women to depressed men at closer to 3:1. Approximately 60 percent of the patients I have treated for depression are women.

There are many factors that may account for this gender difference. Traditionally, in our culture, men are more reluctant to seek medical help, especially psychiatric help, and *especially* for a mood disorder. There may be many depressed men, but they don't usually show up in a doctor's office asking for treatment. Perhaps this is because many of the traditional psychiatric approaches—the so-called "talk therapies"—may not serve men's needs adequately. Many men have not had the social upbringing that helps them recognize and deal with their feelings. Thus therapy aimed at exploring feelings stands a poor chance of working for such individuals, who may respond better to a more active strategy.

Another possible reason more women than men are under treatment for depression is that, despite much progress, women are still disadvantaged in our society. They frequently lack equal power and prestige, and they are sometimes "taught" to be helpless. In some cases these feelings of inadequacy may manifest themselves as clinical depression. Recent data, however, support the fact that men are catching up; today, the ratio of depressed women to depressed men may be closer to 2:1.

At least part of this change may be attributed to a healthy kind of fallout from the women's movement, which encourages men to recognize and respond to their feelings. Recently there have been signs of a growing men's movement that also encourages men to explore the sources of their deeply buried rage. Perhaps, too, society is shedding the stigma attached to depression. More people are realizing that depression is not a moral weakness or a character flaw, but a true biological illness, like diabetes or cancer. Today, *not* getting treatment is seen as the true weakness. Happily, with drugs like Prozac and other antidepressants available, we are able to help more of the people who seek medical attention. In fact, according to Dr. Frederick Goodwin, the administrator of the U.S. Alcohol, Drug Abuse and Mental Health Administration, the treatment of depression is "psychiatry's Number One success story."

WHAT CAUSES DEPRESSION?

In order to understand why medications like Prozac can alleviate depression, it helps to look at the forces that conspire to produce the symptoms of the disorder. But there are limitations here: Nobody can state with utter certainty exactly what causes depression in all cases and under all circumstances. At best we can identify some of the elements that may have some bearing on an individual person, elements that may suggest which treatment approach will work best.

As we proceed, keep in mind that, ultimately, the *cause* of depression is not all that important. When you have a cold, for example, you don't care too much whether you got it from your kids, your boss, or your Great Aunt Tillie. All you *really* care about is how to get relief from the symptoms. The same is true in depression. Too often people, including some physicians, get wrapped up in searching for the cause of someone's depression and, as a result, fail to put enough energy into the search for proper treatment.

The Biological View

You probably know that psychiatrists go through the same rigorous training that all medical doctors undergo. They spend years studying the biological and chemical functioning of the body. As a result they develop an awareness of how a biological breakdown can lead to a variety of illnesses and, more important, how to correct those biological problems. From this biological viewpoint, depression is an illness that in many cases arises primarily from a physical malfunction. While depression is classified as a mental disorder, that doesn't mean depression isn't real or that it is "all in the patient's head." Quite the contrary. An imbalance in the brain's intricate chemistry, a short circuit in its delicate wiring, can produce what Styron called the "howling tempest."

This biological model is supported by the story of Jack, who went through ten years of analysis and was no closer to a solution to his depression. After examining him and diagnosing his depression, I recommended a course of therapy with Prozac. (In medicine, because drugs affect the way the body works, they are considered to be biological treatments.) Within three weeks his depression had lifted. Three weeks—after he had spent ten years and close to $200,000 on analysis. Now that his mood had improved, he no longer even cared whether he had suffered some injury in his childhood. He realized he couldn't go back and undo the past anyway. All that mattered to him was that he felt good *right now*, today, and could finally get on with his life. Yes, he needed some intensive psychotherapy to help him repair the damage that a decade of chronic illness had done to his life. Nonetheless Jack illustrates the two main points of the biological perspective: that the cause of depression is often a biological malfunction, and that the cause is of much less concern—especially to the patient—than its relief.

The Behavioral View

If you eat nothing but junk food, get no sleep, run around naked in the rain, and then play poker for three days with people who have colds, the chances are pretty high that you'll catch a cold (or worse) yourself. By the same token, certain behaviors can trigger a bout of depression.

How can people act to bring on depression? Basically, they do so by giving themselves too little positive self-reinforcement and too much self-punishment. They may set unrealistically high goals for themselves and then suffer serious emotional setbacks when they fail to reach those goals. Instead of enjoying what success they do achieve, they focus on their failures, on the negative things that have happened. Sometimes people interpret a setback as a sign that they have no control over their lives, and thus they begin to feel helpless. (Helplessness is, in fact, one of the key symptoms of depression.) People in such circumstances tend to withdraw from society, becoming more isolated and lonely. Sitting by oneself in a room while all of one's friends are out enjoying themselves is hardly a move calculated to bring joy to life. If this pattern continues, the person is at risk of developing a full-blown case of depression.

When bad habits and faulty behavior produce depressive feelings, the solution is to learn healthier ways of acting. Through behavior modification, people can learn how to avoid harmful actions and reward themselves for doing the right thing. In some cases the use of medications can ease the symptoms so that the person is in a better frame of mind to learn and adopt these new behavioral strategies.

The Cognitive View

Poor behavior can contribute to faulty thinking, but the reverse is also true. Someone who sits home alone on a Saturday night is likely to begin thinking, "I must be unattractive, otherwise I wouldn't be sitting home alone on a Saturday night," and that conclusion leads to increasingly antisocial behavior. Depressive thoughts and images (sometimes called "cognitions") tend to fall into three categories: negative views about the self, negative views about the world, and negative views about the future. "I'm a terrible person, nobody wants to be around me, I'm going to be lonely for the rest of my life."

Often these thoughts, or cognitions, are based on misguided assumptions that these people have somehow rigidly incorporated into their style of thinking. People who feel, for example, that they must *always* get a perfect score on a test or else they will be branded a total failure set themselves up for an unending series of severe emotional blows.

Once on the wrong cognitive track, people are prone to make any number of errors in thinking. Arguing from faulty assumptions ("I never do anything right!"), they will reach "logical" but false conclusions ("Therefore I should do nothing at all!"). Their rigid rule system makes them think they *should* or *must* always act a certain way, and they will feel bad if they violate one of their own rules. They tend to think only in terms of black and white: something is either *totally* good or *totally* bad; there are no shades of gray.

People who adopt this negative style of thinking are susceptible to severe depression. They need help in changing their defective mental programming to look at the world in a more balanced way.

The Interpersonal View

We humans are social creatures. We depend on our contact with other people for emotional as well as physical support. People who are unable to form healthy bonds with others, or whose relationships fail to gratify their needs, sometimes succumb to depression.

One common source of trouble arises when a relationship comes to an end. This can happen a number of ways: through death, separation, divorce, relocation, or changing values. Some people are unable to grieve for their losses in a healthy and positive way. Either they never begin to mourn, or they never stop.

In other cases, people may lack the skills they need to communicate their needs and desires to their partners. Sometimes, too, people have trouble adjusting to changes in their roles in life. Marriage, becoming a parent, promotions—all of these can create disturbances in emotions and behavior. A particularly difficult situation exists when a person lacks the skills needed to establish and nourish healthy relationships with others. Often such people are painfully shy or suffer from some form of personality disorder. Some forms of therapy deal with depression by focusing on a person's difficulty with relationships and teaching new skills for dealing with other people in healthier ways.

The Psychodynamic View

The word *psychodynamic* is based on the Greek words for mind and power and refers to the deeply buried emotional conflicts that affect the way people think and act. This is what most people mean when they refer to the concepts of Freudian analysis, the subconscious, and so on. In this model, depression is seen as the result of unresolved issues, especially those stemming from conflict with one's parents or injuries suffered during the past.

Sometimes, too, people feel intensely angry about something or someone. They may feel powerless to express their feelings directly, perhaps because the target of their anger is an authority figure such as a boss, a spouse, or a parent. They thus turn the anger inward, directing it against themselves. In time such anger can turn into self-loathing, guilt, and eventually depression. The idea behind psychodynamic therapy is that by confronting these ogres from long ago patients will be freed of their invisible bonds.

Other Factors

Evidence continues to mount that at least some forms of mood disorders tend to run in families. This is particularly true of manic depression—alternating periods of depression and elation—and recurring severe depression without episodes of mania. The family histories of depressed people often reveal patterns of substance abuse, personality disorders, or other illnesses such as obsessive-compulsive disorder. We can't yet say whether there is a gene that "causes" depression and that is passed along through the generations. It's more likely that traits carried by several genes can predispose a person to develop a psychiatric illness, which will only erupt if the circumstances are right (or, better said, wrong).

Families can also "infect" their members by their attitudes and behavior. Marital discord, low socioeconomic status, isolation, or poor connections with the outside world can cause people to experience low self-esteem and other depression-like symptoms. Children in households where one or both parents are highly critical, are emotionally withdrawn, or suffer from depression or a related illness are three times as likely to become depressed as children raised in more emotionally stable homes.

Victims of sexual abuse often experience depression. If abuse occurs at an early age, before they are able to understand what is happening, children may experience disturbing feelings that they lack the maturity to handle. As adults such people often suffer from extremely low self-esteem and other depressive symptoms such as fatigue, guilt, or thoughts of suicide.

Sometimes depression can arise as a side effect of illicit drugs or prescription medications: antianxiety drugs such as Valium; antibiotics such as Noroxin; cardiac drugs, including Procardia; anticonvulsants; nonsteroidal anti-inflammatory drugs, and dozens of others. Paradoxically, some antidepressants can lead to a worsening of depressive symptoms.

Chronic illness, including cancer and AIDS, can lead to depression, either as a symptom of the underlying disorder or as a psychological response to the stress of coping with long-term sickness or both.

To paraphrase what they used to say on TV, "Will the real cause of depression please stand up?"

Of course, it is not usually possible to point to one, specific cause. It's more accurate—and clinically more helpful—to state that depression is an intricate complex of symptoms involving biological, psychological, and social elements. For people who are genetically predisposed, a combination of stressful events, past and present, can combine to trigger the onset of depression.

As noted earlier, however, the cause of the problem is of much less concern than the immediate relief of symptoms. When your house is being flooded, you don't start an expedition to locate the source of the river.

SYMPTOMS OF DEPRESSION

Depression involves a range of symptoms. Let's take a look now at what those symptoms are.

As you read this section, remember that all thoughts and feelings are physical signals that travel to, from, and within the brain. The biological chaos that results from depression serves to scramble those circuits, causing the signals to follow strange and unpredictable routes. Like a computer, the brain is built so that it can usually compensate for errors or for strange messages. For example, if you see something that "does not compute," you will blink, rub your eyes, or look away for a moment before deciding that, yes, that really *is* a UFO hovering above the roadway. Depression, however, seems to overpower the "error-correction" systems, leading to faulty "output" in the form of distorted thoughts and emotions.

Sadness

Of course, sad feelings are the sine qua non of depression. To someone in the throes of this illness, nothing seems pleasant, nothing brings joy. Because these feelings are often caused by a physical malfunction, persons who are depressed can't simply "cheer up" or "snap out of it," any more than people can "snap out of" diabetes. One of the cruel things about this illness is that its victims are usually aware of how low they have sunk. They can remember what it was like to feel happy and are convinced that they will never feel that way again, ever. According to the psychiatrist's manual, these sad feelings must be severe enough to disrupt the ability to function and must persist for at least two weeks before an official diagnosis of depression can be made. This criterion helps us recognize those people who have a true illness, as distinct from those who feel "blue" because they are going through a rough time in their lives.

Hopelessness and Helplessness

Virtually all depressed people feel an overwhelming sense of hopelessness and helplessness about their situation. Hope is such a natural human trait that to lose it can be as tragic as losing a limb. As a doctor I know that depression is not hopeless, that there are many effective treatments available. But it can be hard to convince someone who sees the future as bleak and empty that such is the case. Hopelessness puts people in double jeopardy. Not only does it ruin their current outlook; it makes them feel that any attempt to get help or get better is doomed to fail, so they might as well not bother trying.

Because they feel there is no hope, people with depression often feel they are helpless and unable to act to end their misery. Describing his own bout of depression, television personality Dick Cavett said, "What's really diabolical about it is that if there were a pill over there, ten feet from me, that you could guarantee would lift me out of it, it would be too much trouble to go get it."

Loss of Pleasure or Interest in Life

This emotional state is a close cousin of sad feelings and hopelessness. Depressed people no longer take satisfaction in the things they formerly enjoyed: families and friends, jobs, the world around them. Food loses its taste; everything loses its color. I remember one patient who gave away his entire collection of beloved opera records—more than 400 albums—to a church rummage sale because he had completely lost interest in his former consuming passion. William Styron was wryly amused when his doctor warned him that one side effect of his antidepressant medication might be impotence. Styron wondered if the doctor "seriously thought that this juiceless and ravaged semi-invalid with the shuffle and the ancient wheeze woke up each morning from his [drug assisted] sleep eager for carnal fun."

An Overpowering Sense of Guilt and Shame

Guilt is one of the stranger symptoms of depression. Guilt causes people to feel that they are bad or worthless, that they are somehow responsible for their own suffering and for the suffering of others. Sometimes the guilt is so strong that people feel they must punish themselves, an attitude that can interfere with their need to get treatment.

Guilt is essentially a feeling that one has done something wrong. Shame, in contrast, is the feeling that one has hurt or disappointed other people. Depressed persons believe that their illness is somehow the result of a failure on their part and that they have become a burden or an embarrassment to family, friends, or society as a whole. The combined effects of guilt and shame drive many patients to withdraw into the world of their illness and thus make it harder to reach them with treatment.

Feelings of Inadequacy

Low self-esteem shows up as a feeling of utter worthlessness, self-disappointment, or self-loathing. Again, such feelings can make it hard for depressed people to seek help, since they don't feel that they are worth saving. In some cases, the ultimate expression of guilt, hopelessness, and low self-esteem is suicide.

Anxiety

Anxiety produces a sense of dread and apprehension. People with anxiety expect that something horrible is about to happen. They withdraw, preferring to stay home or avoid friends or even abandon their careers rather than risk losing control of themselves. Sometimes the anxiety takes a physical form: sweating, trembling, rapid heartbeat. Anxiety can also be a psychiatric disorder in its own right, one quite distinct from depression and requiring a completely different approach to therapy.

Changes in Appetite

Usually this means eating less—not surprising, since for many people with depression food utterly loses its taste. The biochemical changes caused by the illness may also have some direct impact on the appetite control centers. Often depressed people lose weight, typically around fifteen pounds. In other cases, people develop ravenous appetites, especially for carbohydrates or sweets. Many antidepressant medications list weight gain as a side effect; interestingly, such a gain can help offset the loss caused by the disease and is thus not necessarily bad. As we'll see later, one reason for Prozac's wide appeal is that it rarely promotes weight gain.

Sleep Disturbance

People with depression commonly wake up much too early—at three or four in the morning—and can't get back to sleep. Sometimes people sleep normal hours but their sleep is fitful and does not provide adequate rest. Between 15 and 30 percent of patients sleep too much—up to fourteen hours a day—but never feel rested.

Lethargy

As its name suggests, depression can cause people to slow to a virtual crawl. This loss of energy can make people feel they are living in a kind of suspended animation. They lose the ability to take any action for themselves, whether to eat, get dressed, or get out of bed. Even their speech slows down, becoming monotonous, and filled with long pauses.

Agitation

Conversely, some people experience agitation as a symptom. They can't sit still; they pace, wring their hands, twitch, or wiggle their feet. They may be constantly pulling at their hair or clothing.

Disturbed Thinking

As we have seen, this is a common feature of depression. Patients focus on negative or morbid aspects of life and exaggerate their memories of loss or failure, thus lowering self-esteem even further. Depressed people often become tearful, irritable, and hostile.

Suicidal Feelings

These are, of course, the most serious of all depressive symptoms. Thoughts of suicide are not idle threats; perhaps as many as 15 percent of severely depressed people will kill themselves. Sadly, in some cases, suicide may be the first and only sign that the person was suffering from the disorder. Usually, though, there will be other clues: The person may begin giving away possessions or making remarks like, "Everyone will be happier when I'm gone." *A person experiencing suicidal feelings should get professional help immediately.*

Other symptoms of depression include physical complaints such as headache, stomach ache, fatigue, and muscular ache. In severe cases depression may produce psychosis—hallucinations or delusions of persecution or grandiosity.

TYPES OF DEPRESSION

At first glance, the list of symptoms of depression can seem confusing. Some patients lose weight, others gain it; some have insomnia, others sleep too much; some are agitated, others slow down. How can this be?

The picture becomes clearer when you realize that depression manifests in different disturbed behaviors and feelings, all of which fall into the category known as affective disorders. (Essentially, *affect*—accent on the first syllable—refers to a combination of feelings and thoughts; roughly speaking, it means "mood.") To understand how depression can take many forms, consider pneumonia. Some people who come down with this illness may develop fever and a dry cough. Others may have chest pain and a wet cough but no fever. Similarly, people with depression can manifest widely different combinations of symptoms and still be diagnosed as "depressed." In fact, a person can experience a depressive episode with symptoms A, B, and C, then five years later go through another bout of depression that produces symptoms X, Y, and Z.

The pattern of symptoms depends on many factors, such as the amount of stress coming from the person's environment. Our brains serve as a kind of filter that stands between our bodies and the outside world. The exact structure and stability of that filter can change over time, depending on the way we have been brought up, the experiences we have had, and the things we continue to learn and react to. We will react to a stimulus in different ways under different circumstances. Caught in the throes of depression, some people may not be

---

DEPRESSION CHECKLIST

You may have a clinical depression if you experience five or more of the following symptoms, if those symptoms persist for at least two weeks, and if they interfere with your ability to function.

Appetite changes
Difficulty working
Discouragement about the future
Excessive worry about physical health
Fatigue
Feelings of failure
Feelings of sadness
Feelings of unattractiveness
Frequent crying
Guilty feelings
Irritability
Loss of enjoyment in activities
Loss of interest in other people
Loss of interest in sex
Self-disappointment and self-blame
Sleep disturbances
Suicidal thoughts
Trouble concentrating or making decisions
Weight changes

---

aware—or may be unwilling to admit—that they are ill. That slippery, ever-changing symptom pattern is what makes depression such a frustrating and difficult medical problem, for patients as well as for the physicians who care for them.

Unipolar Depression

One way to conceptualize depression is as a dip in mood that may or may not return to normal. A person plummets into a pit of sadness and despair for a significant period of time. Because this condition involves an emotional shift in only one direction, down, it is known as unipolar ("one pole") depression.

Sometimes a person can have a bout of unipolar depression that persists for a while, lifts, and never returns. We refer to that as a *depressive episode*. If the symptoms are severe, causing serious disruption in the person's ability to function and enjoy life, we will describe that person as suffering from *major depression*.

It may be that depression strikes and never quite goes away, or recurs frequently enough that it seems never to have vanished. The symptoms may be relatively mild; while they don't necessarily keep people from functioning, they are virtually always present and can persist for years. In such cases we will say that the person has *dysthymia*, a word that translates roughly as "disturbed spirit" and refers to a kind of low-frequency emotional rumble. Perhaps four out of a hundred people—more women than men—experience dysthymia.

It's possible for a person with dysthymia to suffer an episode of major depression at the same time—a deep dip on the emotional roller-coaster. Such people are said to have *double depression*.

In most people, depression causes insomnia and loss of appetite. People who experience the opposite pattern—whose depression causes them to eat and sleep more—are said to have *atypical depression*.

Bipolar Depression

The second basic category of affective disorder includes those conditions in which a person alternates between periods of extreme highs and extreme lows. These disorders are called bipolar because the person swings between two emotional poles. A common name for bipolar illness is *manic depression*.

On the surface, it would seem that experiencing an emotional high, or mania, is a kind of relief after the suffering caused by depression. That isn't the case. Mania is a state of hyper-excitement and elation. In the manic phase, people feel expansive, euphoric, on top of the world. Nothing bothers them, even things that *should* bother them. These people experience boundless optimism: "I can do anything and nothing or no one can stop me!" They become hyperactive. They may start an impossible project, change careers, or spend every penny they have in a wild spree. Their thoughts race from topic to topic until their speech becomes impossible to follow. They may go for days without sleep. While mania might seem "fun" for a while, eventually it can cause its victims to become irritable and angry. Sometimes they may take dangerous chances, such as driving too fast or abusing drugs or alcohol, with disastrous results.

Mania can last as long as three exhausting months. Then, as suddenly as if someone had flipped a light switch, the person can plunge into the darkness of the depressive phase. As you can imagine, being jerked from one extreme to the other can take a severe toll, emotionally and physically. Generally manic depressives experience a period of normal mood between their highs and lows. In some cases, however, they go from one to the other without a break. It may happen that the cycle repeats itself within the course of an exhausting few days; such people are termed *rapid cyclers*.

Manic depression strikes perhaps 1 percent of the population. While major (unipolar) depression can crop up at any point in life, bipolar disorders tend to emerge before the age of thirty-five. Men are as likely to become manic as women, whereas more women experience major depression than men.

Seasonal Affective Disorders (SAD)

Within the past few years psychiatrists have officially recognized the existence of a type of bipolar mood problem known as *seasonal affective disorder*, or, appropriately, SAD. People with SAD usually start to feel depressed during the autumn, when the days grow shorter. Their low mood persists throughout the winter and only begins to lift with the arrival of spring. Some people soar through the sunny months in a kind of near-manic state, known as hypomania ("low high"). Then, as the leaves turn again, so does their mood.

People with SAD are extremely sensitive to the amount of light they are exposed to during the course of the day. Light acts as a kind of signal that helps the brain coordinate the production of various chemicals regulating mood and other body functions. Research suggests that sunlight tells the brain to stop producing a hormone known as melatonin. At night, with the onset of darkness, melatonin production begins again. Among its other jobs, melatonin is involved in mood control. For some people, too much darkness may mean their bodies produce too much melatonin, which leads to persistent feelings of depression.

The treatment for SAD is simple, cheap, safe, and effective: light. During the winter months patients sit for thirty minutes to two hours or more in front of a box that emanates a special light that approximates the spectrum of light from the sun. The difference it makes can be astounding. People who before dreaded the arrival of winter, hated Christmas, and made themselves and their families miserable can now enjoy themselves and their lives year-round. Some people, however, learning that sunlight is the cure, prefer to move to a southern latitude.

IS IT REALLY DEPRESSION?

Sometimes what appears to be depression is actually some other medical condition entirely. The list of "mimicks" is a long one: hormonal and metabolic disorders, such as thyroid malfunction or diabetes; infectious diseases such as the flu or mononucleosis; cancer; neurological diseases such as Parkinson's or certain forms of epilepsy; blood diseases such as anemia; even poisoning from mercury or other metals. An overactive thyroid can produce a syndrome that closely resembles mania: hyperactivity, sleeplessness, and so on. Conversely, a sluggish thyroid can lead to fatigue, lethargy, and disturbed sleep.

A physician is trained to examine patients thoroughly before arriving at a diagnosis. It would be bad medicine to prescribe an antidepressant when the problem is a malfunctioning thyroid, for example. A doctor would be putting patients at risk if they complained of depression and the doctor failed to screen for cancer or other illnesses that can produce similar symptoms.

When seeking medical care, most people start with a visit to their family physician, general practitioner, or internist. Recently, however, a study found that physicians who have not received special training in psychiatric disorders may fail to recognize depression perhaps as much as 50 percent of the time. Sometimes, too, physicians may tend to stick with strategies that worked for them in the past; they thus may be unfamiliar with—or unwilling to prescribe—newer medications. In seeking treatment, don't hesitate to ask about your doctor's qualifications. Ideally doctors will refer patients to specialists, such as a psychiatrist, if the diagnosis seems to lie outside their area of expertise.

However, once the presence of depression is confirmed and the physician has determined that the problem does not arise from a temporary stressful situation, the decision on what treatment to use can be made. Fortunately, depression is one of the most treatable psychiatric illnesses, and as we'll see in the next chapter, there are many effective strategies available.

GETTING BETTER ALL THE TIME:

DRUG TREATMENT FOR DEPRESSION

Medicine truly is as much an art as it is a science. All art involves some degree of interpretation. A painter interprets the landscape in terms of colors and brushstrokes; a composer interprets emotion in terms of rhythm and tone. Similarly, a doctor—a good one, anyway—listens to what the patient is saying and feeling. The doctor then interprets the situation so as to choose the type of therapy that has the best chance of doing the patient the most good.

All treatment involves some degree of risk. There is, of course, the risk that the choice of treatment will be ineffective and that the illness will persist or become worse. There is also the risk that the treatment itself will cause problems; that's what is meant by side effects. In making choices, doctors weigh the possible benefits of treatment against the potential risks. If in their interpretation the good outweighs the harm, then they proceed with caution, and will continue to monitor the patient's progress to watch for any signs of trouble.

Three decades ago depression was seen as a devastating condition that stubbornly resisted most efforts at treatment. Today, however, we know that, while depression is still a serious illness, as many as eight out of ten depressed people can get effective relief—providing their doctors interpret their needs correctly.

The difference in the success rate is largely due to two parallel trends. First, as we might expect, scientists today have a much clearer understanding of how the brain works than they did thirty-five years ago. While there is still a lot to be learned, recent discoveries have revealed the brain to be extraordinarily sensitive to the slightest shifts in the biochemical balance. We are also aware that this biochemical system is highly complex, and that many factors—from diet to the humidity of the air—can upset the balance. The other main trend has been the discovery of medications that are designed, with increasingly greater precision, to correct specific imbalances.

BIOLOGY, THE BRAIN, AND THE BLUES

The nerve cells in the brain are separated by tiny gaps. Neurotransmitters carry signals across these gaps. Without these chemical messengers, signals can't travel and the brain loses power. The communication network breaks down.

Neurotransmitter molecules all have precise shapes. Just as a key fits into the ignition switch on your car, these shapes fit snugly into certain areas known as receptors found on the surfaces of other cells. When the key is inserted, the cell's "ignition" fires up and the message continues on its way. Problems such as depression can arise if not enough neurotransmitters are in circulation or if they aren't able to make their way to the receptors.

One day in the late 1950s, some Swiss scientists, searching for a cure for the common cold, stumbled across a new chemical. This compound didn't help colds at all. What it did, however, was even more remarkable. The new drug, called imipramine, boosted neurotransmitter levels, which gave it the potential to help the brain's emotional motor work more normally. A few years later, the first antidepressant available as a prescription drug was born.

Previously, the only drugs prescribed for depression were stimulants such as amphetamines. Stimulants speed things up, which sometimes relieves the general slowing down depression can cause, but they don't really change the underlying mood.

Imipramine boosts the supply of two neurotransmitters, norepinephrine and serotonin. With imipramine we entered the age of biopsychiatry. Other drugs were soon created that affected different brain systems in different ways, yet still produced an antidepressant effect. Results of using these new drugs showed that the neurotransmitter systems were far more numerous, complex, and interconnected than was at first believed.

THE TRICYCLICS

Imipramine is called a "tricyclic" drug because its molecules are shaped like three rings linked together. Other tricyclic antidepressants (TCA's) soon followed. The people who seem to respond best to TCA's are those whose depression produces clear physical symptoms: disturbed sleep, appetite changes, and so on.

Once a neurotransmitter has been released and has carried its message to the other cell, one of two things happens. In some cases an enzyme breaks the neurotransmitter down into smaller parts that are eventually flushed out of the body. Otherwise the neurotransmitter is reabsorbed by the cells and stored for later use, a kind of biological recycling process known as "reuptake."

ANTIDEPRESSANTS

Type of drug	Generic name	Brand name
Stimulants	amphetamine	Dexedrine
	methylphenidate	Ritalin
Tricyclics (TCA's)	amitriptyline	Elavil
	amoxapine	Asendin
	clomipramine	Anafranil
	desipramine	Norpramine
	doxepin	Sinequan
	imipramine	Tofranil
	nortriptyline	Pamelor
	protriptyline	Vivactil
	trimipramine	Surmontil
Monoamine Oxidase Inhibitors (MAOI's)	isocarboxazid	Marplan
	phenelzine sulfate	Nardil
	tranylcypromine	Parmate
Aminoketone	bupropion	Wellbutrin
Atypical	trazodone	Desyrel
Serotonin reuptake inhibitor	fluoxetine	Prozac

The TCA's are effective drugs, but as with many medications, their effects can go beyond the problem they are intended to address. Instead of blocking reuptake of just one specific neurotransmitter, TCA's prevent the reabsorption of several neurotransmitters, including serotonin and norepinephrine. That's not all they do. Like chemical gate-crashers, some TCA's can also muscle their way into a number of different cell receptors. These drugs then jam the receptors with their own chemical keys, which *prevent* the receptor's ignition switch from firing, and thus block signals from traveling through the cell. The more receptor systems affected by these drugs, the more impact they have on the body.

This is why such drugs often do what we want them to—relieve depression, for example—but produce a lot of unwanted side effects as well. These are covered in Chapter 3.

THE MAOI'S

The neurotransmitters serotonin, dopamine, and nor-epinephrine are all members of a group scientists call the monoamines. The enzyme that breaks these monoamines into smaller pieces, thereby hindering neurotransmission, is called monoamine oxidase, or MAO for short.

Certain chemicals can block the MAO enzyme from breaking down monoamine molecules. Like chemical soldiers, these drugs defend the body's monoamine supply by stopping (or, as scientists say, inhibiting) the enzymes from destroying neurotransmitters. With these protective chemicals patrolling the neighborhood, more neurotransmitters are kept in circulation to connect with receptors. More connections means more relief of depression. In the early 1960s a group of antidepressants that work this way, the monoamine oxidase inhibitors (MAOI's) came on the scene.

The MAOI's pose a big problem, however. They stop monoamine oxidase from doing its *other* main job, which is to break down a molecule called tyramine. Tyramine can affect blood pressure. You consume a lot of tyramine when you eat such foods as aged cheese, beer, wine, pickled herring, chicken liver, yeast, coffee, broad-bean pods, and canned figs. After eating these foods, tyramine molecules swarm into the brain. Normally the MAO enzymes keep tyramine in check. But people taking MAOI's put their enzymes out of commission and are thus at risk of having their blood pressure shoot up to dangerously high levels.

There are other complications. MAOI's can cause damage to the liver, brain, and cardiovascular system, and in overdose could produce hallucinations, fever, and convulsions. Some early brands of MAOI's were proved so dangerous that they were taken off the market.

In the past decade or so, however, MAOI's have come back into favor. We now understand the tyramine problem and, by warning patients to follow tyramine-free diets, can pretty much avoid the risk. Also, some people who don't respond to any other medications do improve when using MAOI's. These drugs are thus the only hope some people have of finding relief for their depression.

LITHIUM

Yet another lucky discovery was the fact that a salt known as lithium carbonate could relieve the mania seen in bipolar disorders. The first clue came from an experiment in which guinea pigs given lithium became lethargic. That wasn't exactly what the researcher, an Australian named John F. Cade, was looking for in the late 1940s, but he settled for it when he realized lithium might help the mentally ill.

No one took much notice of his published report, however, and the use of lithium in manic depression had to wait until Cade's work was rediscovered twenty years later. We know now that lithium can help perhaps 70 percent of manic-depressive patients in their manic phase. There is no way to reckon the amount of misery this relatively simple drug has spared the world.

ENTER PROZAC

As research progressed, scientists realized that the brain is awash in neurotransmitters. Picture the brain as a plumbing system like your bathroom sink, but instead of just hot and cold faucets, there are dozens of faucets, one for each of the neurotransmitters. You can turn the knobs to release more neurotransmitters or turn them to produce less. You can have several of these taps running at the same time. Some neurotransmitters eventually get sucked down the drain and are flushed from the body. Others get pumped back into the system to be used again.

Now, if your bathroom faucet develops an annoying drip, you don't call in the plumber to rip out all the pipes in your house. Ideally, all you need to do is insert a new washer in the faucet. The same principle applies to medicine. If there's a problem with one neurotransmitter system, you don't need a drug that affects a whole bunch of them.

In some cases of depression, the problem may arise from an insufficient supply of the neurotransmitter serotonin. In the mid-1970s scientists discovered a chemical that works like a highly specialized plumber whose only job is to prevent cells from reabsorbing the molecules of serotonin. This increases the amount of serotonin at nerve endings. What's more, unlike the TCA's, this same drug is highly selective: It affects serotonin but apparently leaves the other neurotransmitter systems alone. This drug, the first in a new classification called serotonin reuptake inhibitors, eventually made it to the marketplace.

Doctors know it as fluoxetine. You know it as Prozac.

SEROTONIN: A CLOSER LOOK

The neurotransmitter serotonin was discovered a century ago. Since then researchers have found evidence suggesting (but by no means proving) that serotonin may play an important role in a huge number of bodily processes and psychiatric conditions. So many jobs have been ascribed to serotonin that it probably functions more as an intermediary in the brain—a chemical "supervisor" rather than a hands-on laborer.

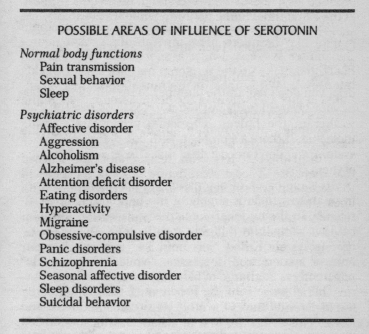

POSSIBLE AREAS OF INFLUENCE OF SEROTONIN

Normal body functions
   Pain transmission
   Sexual behavior
   Sleep

Psychiatric disorders
   Affective disorder
   Aggression
   Alcoholism
   Alzheimer's disease
   Attention deficit disorder
   Eating disorders
   Hyperactivity
   Migraine
   Obsessive-compulsive disorder
   Panic disorders
   Schizophrenia
   Seasonal affective disorder
   Sleep disorders
   Suicidal behavior

In order to manufacture serotonin, brain cells need a good supply of an amino acid called tryptophan. The body gets its tryptophan from certain foods such as milk, poultry, eggs, red meats, and nuts. Until recently, many health food stores sold tryptophan as a dietary supplement. (Tryptophan made the news because some people taking it as a supplement developed a potentially fatal blood disorder. It turned out that pure tryptophan made by a chemical company for inclusion in tryptophan tablets had been tainted during the manufacturing process. The FDA has banned the sale of tryptophan supplements pending the outcome of its review. While tryptophan is a necessary component of a healthy diet, you should always consult with a doctor pharmacist, or, perhaps even better, a nutritionist who keeps up with the latest developments, before taking any food supplements.)

Recent brain research suggests that the serotonin system may be much more intricate than other neurotransmitter systems. Under a microscope the cells and fibers that make up the serotonin network appear thickly interwoven. While most neurotransmitters are concentrated in just a few areas of the brain, serotonin-secreting cells are woven into the brain at many strategic locations. For example, the serotonin supply is plentiful in the limbic region of the brain, which regulates emotions.

Within the last few years researchers have learned that there are at least six different types of receptors in the serotonin system, not just one. Like the various train lines that make up a subway network, each of these receptors may be responsible for transmitting different types of signals to different destinations. For example, the subsystem called "serotonin 1A" may regulate our level of anxiety and depression, while "serotonin 1D" apparently is in charge of blood vessel constriction.

This glimpse into the functioning brain shows why scientists continue to search for drugs with more and more precise mechanisms of action. A drug that affects only one serotonin subsystem and leaves all the others alone will produce more specific and predictable therapeutic effects and fewer side effects. The evidence shows Prozac to be such a drug.

It's important to note, however, that we are still in the Dark Ages when it comes to understanding the neurotransmitter system. It may turn out that blocking serotonin reuptake directly relieves depression. Or, it may be true that tweaking the serotonin knob(s) results in tiny changes in other neurotransmitter systems, and *those* changes may actually produce the antidepressant effect. We simply don't know, but the evidence that serotonin helps regulate mood, in the words of one scientist, is "robust." There are also many signs that a defective serotonin system may show up in other physical and psychiatric problems: compulsive behavior, such as that seen in eating disorders, alcoholism, and obsessive-compulsive disorder, as well as impulsive behavior such as violence and suicide. In the near future we may have simple lab tests that will identify serotonin malfunctions and thus identify people at greatest risk. We may also be able to choose treatments precisely targeted to correct certain chemical imbalances. By recognizing the prime candidates for serotonin drugs in advance, we may become more able to prevent many personal tragedies.

CAUTIONS WHEN CONSIDERING DRUG THERAPIES

In all fields of medicine, but especially psychiatry, the use of drugs for treatment raises a number of concerns, not just about safety and efficacy, but about ethical issues. What follows is a discussion of some of those questions.

Safety

The process of drug discovery and approval takes years. Pharmaceutical manufacturers must gather vast amounts of data to prove to the Food and Drug Administration that their product not only does what is promised, but does so in an acceptably safe way.

In debating the question of safety, many people overlook a key fact: *No drug is completely safe*. Many drugs are lethal if taken incorrectly or in great amounts. People have died from allergic reactions to such "harmless" drugs as penicillin and aspirin. Nonetheless, the power of such drugs to relieve suffering in millions of people is so tremendous that to take them off the market would border on cruelty.

Side Effects

A side effect may be defined simply as an unwanted drug effect. Any drug may cause side effects in some individuals. Often people are willing to tolerate the side effects because the relief of their symptoms is worth the inconvenience. The debate over how to use medications in light of their side effects rages continuously in the countless pages of thousands of medical journals published around the world.

The side effects typically seen with TCA's include sedation, weight gain, dry mouth, blurred vision, dizziness, constipation, rapid pulse, and difficulty urinating. Some people experience a decrease in their sexual drive, while others report an increase. Rarely, men may report swelling of the testicles or of the breasts, while women may notice breast enlargement or secretion of milk.

Side effects of MAOI's may include headaches, nausea, vomiting, rapid or irregular heartbeat, stiff neck, dilated pupils, or sudden sensitivity to light. Some people taking MAOI's experience dizziness, especially when they stand up quickly. MAOI's can cause impotence in some men.

The unique antidepressant bupropion (Wellbutrin) may cause agitation, dry mouth, nausea with or without vomiting, sweating, weight change, dizziness, headache, insomnia, and blurred vision. While painful erections and delayed ejaculations occurred in less than 1 percent of people taking bupropion, impotence or decreased sexual drive were reported by 3 percent.

Trazodone (Desyrel) is also a one-of-a-kind drug, with a slightly different side effect profile. Trazodone can cause drowsiness, nervousness, dizziness, dry mouth, fatigue, headache, insomnia, and nausea.

Fluoxetine (Prozac) has garnered much of its publicity because it is often perceived to be freer from side effects. This image does not quite hold up under scrutiny. Like all drugs, Prozac has its down side. Typical side effects include nausea, headache, anxiety, and insomnia. Prozac is reported to cause decreased sexual urges in 1.6 percent of people taking the drug. Close to 2 percent may experience sexual dysfunction, specifically loss or delay of orgasm. The next chapter offers more detail about these potential problems and explains why many people feel that the benefits from the drug offset the complications. In Chapter 6 we'll also scrutinize the reports suggesting that Prozac can trigger suicidal or otherwise violent behavior.

Slow Response Time

Take an aspirin for a headache or a Valium for anxiety and you notice the effect almost instantly. Not so with antidepressants. There can be a lag from three weeks to two months before they begin working. Apparently it takes that long for the drugs to produce a significant impact on the neurotransmitter systems. Some patients may wait a month or so and complain that the drug isn't working. We may then switch drugs, only to learn that the first drug *would* have worked if we'd only given it a little more time. For someone who is stuck in the stultifying prison of depression, the delay before an antidepressant begins to work can be agonizing.

Compliance

The term *compliance* is used to describe how well people comply with their doctors' directions for use. Do they take it according to directions? If the side effects are particularly severe, many patients will stop using the drug. Then there's no chance at all that the drug will do any good. Some other medications cause problems because they must be taken two, three, or four times a day, or at awkward times during the day. The easier it is to remember to take the medicine, the more likely people are to use it. (One advantage of Prozac is that it is usually taken only once in the day, rather than at intervals throughout the day.)

Overdose

Overdose is of special concern in depression, since many of its victims may attempt suicide. It's not uncommon for depressed people to hoard their pills until they have collected a lethal dose. We can't yet predict which patients will attempt to kill themselves, but, as we saw in Chapter 1, there may be warning signs. The tricyclic antidepressants can be fatal in overdose, causing nearly forty deaths for every one million prescriptions. Newer categories of drugs appear to be somewhat safer than the older ones such as the TCA's. There are very few reports of toxic overdose with Prozac; patients who have ingested large doses usually escape with nothing more serious than a stomach ache.

Relapse

Depression is a damnable condition in part because it is highly likely to return. Some people may go for years between episodes; for other people the interval can be measured in weeks or even days. We still lack the hard data on how long people should keep taking antidepressants once their mood has lifted. As a rule, I ask my patients to keep using their medication for six months or a year after symptoms clear. The trouble is, when people finally feel better they tend to think they no longer need the support of the drug, so they stop taking it. That's the compliance problem I mentioned a moment ago. I follow up with my patients each month to make sure they're using the medicine properly and are not experiencing symptoms that signal the start of a relapse.

Preventing Depression

Lithium is quite good at preventing people from going into a manic state. Antidepressants such as the tricyclics, however, can have the opposite effect, and are not used as a preventive measure in people with bipolar disorders. Conversely, lithium isn't reliable at preventing bouts of unipolar depression, but, as noted above, the other anti-depressants should be used for months after the person's mood lifts. Doctors want their patients to continue living as normal a life as possible while their treatment proceeds. Ideally, however, the goal of any therapy, whether it involves drugs or psychotherapy or both, is to return people to their normal lives without the need for further treatment. If, however, symptoms reappear after the person stops using the drug, then the physician is likely to renew the prescription.

Drugs and Older Adults

As a rule, older adults break down drugs in their bodies differently than younger adults. What's more, they are often taking several drugs at the same time because they may suffer from more than one condition. The interactions among these drugs may be unpredictable. Because of their social and economic conditions, some older people trying to cope with long-term illness are at especially high risk of suicide. The long lag time between taking antidepressants and feeling their effects is particularly troublesome for the elderly, who may feel they don't have much time left anyway.

Social Concerns

Strangely, in our society people who are strong enough to seek help for their psychiatric problems are sometimes condemned as "weak" by thoughtless others. No one would criticize a person who gets treatment for diabetes as being "weak." Yet some people still perceive mental illness as a character flaw. However, as the biological research outlined above shows, these are often physical illnesses that can be treated through physical means.

As a culture we must end the stigma attached to depression and other psychiatric disorders.

Fortunately, there are signs of hope. In 1972 Thomas Eagleton was dumped as George McGovern's vice-presidential running mate when it was revealed that he had undergone electroconvulsive therapy for depression. In 1990, however, Lawton Chiles was elected governor of Florida *despite* his controversial and well-publicized admission that he was taking Prozac. Maybe we're beginning to see that people who get help when they need it are actually smarter than those who don't.

Psychological Concerns

Some people decry medicines as a kind of crutch. Actually, they *are* a crutch. A crutch is something that temporarily takes the pressure off a wounded area to give it a chance to heal. By alleviating the incapacitating sadness of depression, medications can give people an emotional "breather" and make things easier for them as they get their lives back on track. If I believe a medicine will help someone, and if that person refuses to take the drug, I will wonder if this patient is using the illness as an excuse for not getting better. I can understand when someone tells me, "I'm afraid of drugs" or "I feel any change has to come from within, not as something from outside me." I try to reassure people that, ideally, drugs do nothing more than correct imperfections in the brain's basic structure and help the brain return to its normal functioning.

The "Center Effect"

People often dredge up a supposedly scientific study to prove that such-and-such a medication does or does not cause such-and-such an effect. When such studies present conclusions that go against the grain of common sense, it's best to view them with a healthy and scientifically appropriate skepticism. Different treatment centers develop personalities of their own. The directors of such centers, and some of the people who work for them, may have their own biases for or against the use of medication. This is what I mean by the "center effect." If researchers at a center do not wholeheartedly accept the use of medications, they can sometimes communicate that attitude to the people taking part in a study. Not many patients will enthusiastically comply with a drug regimen if their doctors say, "Well, you can take this medication, but it probably won't do you much good, and it could even do you harm." Poor compliance will lead to skewed and misleading results.

OTHER TREATMENT OPTIONS

This is primarily a book about a new antidepressant drug and how it compares to other available medications. I only have space to mention briefly some of the other kinds of treatment available for depression.

Talk Therapy

The so-called "talk therapies" can make a big difference in how people manage their illness. Behavioral therapy offers practical suggestions on how to reinforce healthy behavior through a system of self-rewards. Cognitive therapy identifies the troubled patterns of thinking that can lead to depressive attitudes. Interpersonal therapy concentrates on ways to improve faulty or unfulfilling relationships. Psychodynamic therapy resembles classical psychoanalysis in that it explores the past for signs of unresolved emotional conflict. In psychodynamic therapy, however, the therapist tends to take a more active role in directing the discussion and in offering suggestions or interpretations.

In essence, therapy is anything you do to help yourself feel better. Talking to another person who understands your problem and can suggest strategies for improvement can be a vital part of the healing process. Learning about the illness is another important step. Any of these methods may work, depending on several factors: the patient's needs and interests, the severity of symptoms, the skills of the caregiver.

We now know that people with depression don't have to undergo years of psychoanalysis. Short-term psychotherapy—perhaps as little as six to sixteen weeks—may be enough to turn the patient's life around. Some people do well in individual therapy, where they meet one-on-one with the physician, psychologist, or social worker. Others benefit by being in a therapy group and learning from other patients how to cope with, and overcome, their illness. In some cases family therapy, marital therapy, or other types of help may be needed. There is no "one-size-fits-all" treatment; each person is unique, and each case has different requirements.

Is psychotherapy effective? Yes, but only recently have these strategies been subjected to the same type of rigorous study as medical treatment. We now have strong scientific evidence that psychotherapy does indeed work. One study, for example, reports that psychotherapy for psychiatric disorders is the equivalent of reducing the rate of a given illness from 66 percent to 34 percent. Another study found that, overall, patients with serious psychiatric problems who underwent psychotherapy improved from an average rating of 50 to 77 on a scale of 100. Both of these findings are statistically significant.

Combination Therapy

Frequently, depressed people do well when drug therapy is used in conjunction with some form of talk therapy. The drugs take some of the "heat" out of the emotional system and make it possible for people to take part in, and thus benefit from, the other techniques.

A recent study by the National Institute of Mental Health found that patients with depression improved after sixteen weeks of treatment with two forms of "talk therapy"—interpersonal and cognitive. The greatest improvement, however, was seen among those who had a combination of psychotherapy plus an antidepressant (in this study, imipramine).

Exercise

Figuratively speaking, scientists have finally caught up with joggers, who have long known that exercise can profoundly improve their mood. There is now solid evidence that vigorous aerobic exercise such as running, swimming, or biking produces changes in the body's neurotransmitter systems, including serotonin. Exercise also builds up resistance to stress and improves the body's ability to withstand the many shocks, small and large, to which it is subjected during the course of a day, thus reducing the impact of depression.

In a recent study, people with depression who exercised showed a significant decrease in their symptoms over those in a control group who did not exercise. Some experts feel that even a brisk ten- or twenty-minute walk during the middle of the day can be highly therapeutic. In addition to the physical benefits of exercise, there are psychological ones as well. Physical fitness can reduce shyness and social isolation, improve self confidence, self-esteem, and the feeling of self-mastery, improve memory and reasoning ability, reduce reaction time, and boost the ability to concentrate and make decisions.

Electric Shock Treatment

In severe cases electroconvulsive therapy (ECT) may work where nothing else has succeeded. The way ECT is administered today bears very little resemblance to the "torture-chamber" image it earned in earlier decades, such as was depicted in the movie *One Flew Over the Cuckoo's Nest*. Still, some people may experience some memory loss following a series of ECT treatments.

Surgery

Lobotomy, a procedure in which surgeons sever some of the faulty connections in the brain, is rarely used today. A related but very rare procedure is the cingulotomy, which severs a tiny bundle of nerves that links the emotional centers and the thought centers of the brain. Unlike lobotomy, cingulotomy, which is used to treat severely depressed or obsessed individuals, apparently does not affect the patient's intellect or personality.

In choosing treatment, I select the method that stands the best chance of producing the greatest benefit in the shortest amount of time. In many cases, that means reaching for my prescription pad.

A DOCTOR LOOKS
AT PROZAC

Doctors often refer jokingly to "Hawthorne's Law": Prescribe a drug only when it's new, because that's when it works.

There are fads in medicine, just as there are fads in fashion and music. Drug makers release their new products in a flurry of publicity. The media, eager to fill space and kill time, willingly grab the bait. The first reports trumpet fabulous success stories: "Medical Breakthrough!" "New Drug Banishes the Blues!"

Of course, it isn't long before some people who try the drug find they aren't getting the relief they thought they'd been promised. Reports of side effects trickle in. Ominous grumblings are heard. The drug that held such promise may not be the cure-all it was touted to be. In some cases drug makers, socked with lawsuits, consider withdrawing a product from the market, even though the medication—properly prescribed and properly used—might have helped millions.

The careers of many drugs follow an arc from wild enthusiasm to total damnation. Fortunately, rational thinking usually prevails as we learn more about how to use the drug and for which patients.

Prozac seems to be following the standard career track for a new medicine. Enthusiasm for Prozac was so high that by the fall of 1990, roughly 800,000 prescriptions were being written each month; worldwide sales were estimated at nearly $700 million. The initial flurry of excitement may have led some physicians to prescribe the drug for patients who didn't really need it. By the end of 1990—predictably—the pendulum began swinging the other way, propelled by a few sketchy reports of adverse reactions. Sales fell, confusion rose.

This book offers some perspective on the Prozac puzzle and tries to restores a little order to the sometimes chaotic debate. Let's start by showing how doctors size up Prozac, as they would any new drug. Some of the following may be a bit technical in spots. Basically, all we are doing is reviewing the reports on Prozac that have appeared over the last few years and assessing the value of their findings.

PROZAC IN THE BODY

In the previous chapter we saw how antidepressant drugs seem to work by adjusting the balance of chemical messengers in the brain. As you'll recall, some antidepressants affect several neurotransmitters at one time. Prozac, however, is highly selective. It prevents nerve endings in the brain from reabsorbing serotonin but apparently has no impact on other neurotransmitter systems. This selectivity may offer a real advantage, since the drug doesn't attempt to fix parts of the brain that aren't necessarily "broken."

Let's take a moment to explain why we use words like *apparently* and *seems* in describing these drugs. We know antidepressants improve mood, but we don't know exactly how they do it. Much of the scientific evidence that antidepressants affect neurotransmitter systems comes from test-tube experiments. We don't yet have the tools we need to peer inside the living human brain and observe drug molecules at work. Nor do we know whether the drugs might be causing other subtle changes that we don't happen to be looking for at the time. Picture the brain as a bowl of spaghetti. If you pull out one strand, the other strands shift around a little in unpredictable ways. The changes that result will be different each time you remove a strand. Using a drug like Prozac to change the serotonin system may cause the other brain "strands" to adjust. Exactly which of those adjustments is the one that lifts the person out of depression remains to be seen.

Although we can't directly observe Prozac at work, we can find indirect clues that tell us what's happening. For example, we know that 75 percent of a dose of Prozac eventually passes from the body in the urine, and another 10 percent is passed in the feces.

By tracking Prozac's passage, we know that the body takes a relatively long time to break down fluoxetine, the active ingredient, compared to other drugs. One measure scientists use is the time it takes for half of a dose of a drug to be metabolized; this is known as the drug's half-life. The elimination half-life of Prozac—the time it takes for half of a dose to pass through—is one to three days.

Fluoxetine molecules are chopped up by enzymes in the liver. The main product left over after this process is completed is known as norfluoxetine. Interestingly, norfluoxetine also appears to block serotonin reuptake. Thus, even though fluoxetine molecules have been broken into pieces, some of those pieces continue to affect the serotonin system and contribute to the drug's antidepressant effect. (Not all drugs produce such "active metabolites.") Norfluoxetine has an even longer elimination half-life than its parent fluoxetine; it can take as long as seven to fifteen days for half the amount of norfluoxetine to pass. For comparison, the liver metabolizes an ounce of alcohol in about two hours.

Knowing the half-life is important because it affects the way doctors prescribe a drug. Fluoxetine's long half-life means the drug can usually be given once a day, which makes compliance easier. We have to adjust the daily dosage to allow for the fact that both fluoxetine and its metabolite float around for weeks doing their job. The goal is to reach what we call "steady state." Steady state is the point at which each day's dose replaces the amount of fluoxetine lost in the past twenty-four hours and thus maintains a steady and predictable therapeutic effect. Some Prozac will remain in the body for days, even weeks, after the last dose has been taken. Anyone who experiences an unpleasant side effect or who reacts to a combination of Prozac and some other drug needs to be aware that such problems may persist for a little while until the body has had time to eliminate the medication.

WHO SHOULD TAKE PROZAC—AND HOW?

When I first meet a patient, before making any treatment decision, I ask a lot of questions. We may talk for hours before I'm satisfied that this person does have an illness treatable by medication and that Prozac is a reasonable choice in this case.

Prozac has been officially approved by the FDA only for the treatment of depression. (Chapter 4 discusses other conditions where it may also be of use.) But depression comes in different shapes and sizes. Even if a patient is clearly depressed, the physician will need to dig deeper to find out what subspecies of depression is involved. That means asking the patient about the symptoms experienced. If a patient is experiencing psychotic events—having hallucinations, hearing voices, or feeling paranoid—the treatment of choice is probably a tricyclic antidepressant taken along with an antipsychotic medicine. For many patients, depression causes insomnia. In those circumstances the patient may do better on a drug that helps promote sleep. The same is true in cases where severe anxiety is involved, although one study found that even anxious patients can experience relief with Prozac.

Many doctors consider Prozac as a first choice for patients who are depressed, whose sleep is normal, and who need to be able to function during the day. They may also give the drug to people who previously didn't do as well on tricyclic antidepressants as was hoped, or who had trouble putting up with the side effects. Prozac is often the first choice for depressed people who also have weight problems or who experience obsessions. Studies have found that people with atypical depression—whose symptoms include overeating or oversleeping—respond better to Prozac than to TCA's such as imipramine.

The use of psychiatric medications in children is controversial. It can be hard to diagnose depression in young people, since their bodies and minds are changing so rapidly and so dramatically. In cases where the presence of depression is clear, however, Prozac is a reasonable choice. Prozac does not pose the risk of cardiovascular and other side effects such as dry mouth, constipation, and weight gain that generally rule out the use of TCA's such as imipramine or desipramine. These effects are hard on adults; they can be even harder on children and adolescents. There are also reports that Prozac effectively reduces the symptoms of obsessive-compulsive disorder, which often strikes people as young as ten years old. Some patients with bulimia, many of whom are teenagers, also respond to the drug.

Recently researchers have found that very often clinical depression in older individuals goes unnoticed, and is thus untreated, because the symptoms are confused with other illnesses such as Alzheimer's disease. Prozac is a reasonable option for treating older patients, who are often unable to tolerate the side effects associated with the TCA's. Older patients may be able to use less of the medication and still notice improvement in their depression. Some reports note that use of Prozac may cause some older individuals to experience decreased levels of sodium in the bloodstream, which can lead to water retention and swelling (edema). Also, many older patients are taking a number of other medications, some of which may interact adversely with an antidepressant. Like all medications, Prozac must be used with caution in the elderly.

At all times the physician must listen to the patient's concerns about medication and then respond accordingly. For example, many patients are aware that the tricyclics can promote weight gain. Research indicates that Prozac can help patients suppress appetite and thus avoid weight gain. If patients seem troubled by this potential problem—if extra poundage may contribute to the severity of their depression—then the physician may well consider Prozac.

People taking Prozac or any antidepressant need to be warned about some possible complications. For example, they shouldn't drive or operate hazardous machinery until they have been taking the drug for at least two weeks without noticing any adverse effects. They should continue to watch for signs that the drug may be causing drowsiness. Any drug that affects the brain may impair judgment, thinking, or muscle control. Also, a physician should have a complete list of all the other drugs the patient is taking to look for any possible drug interactions. Patients should avoid alcohol or over-the-counter drugs and let their doctors know if they might become pregnant or are breast-feeding an infant during the course of therapy.

WHO SHOULD NOT TAKE PROZAC?

According to the official prescribing literature, the only people who should not take Prozac are those who are known to be allergic (or "hypersensitive") to the medication. Of course, the only way really to know if people are allergic is for them to take the drug and see if a problem develops.

People who are currently taking Prozac should wait at least five weeks before beginning therapy with an MAOI antidepressant. The drugs could interact in potentially serious ways, and the combination can even be fatal. The same caution must be applied to any patient taking one or more other drugs.

Patients who develop a rash—approximately 4 percent of people taking Prozac—should notify their physicians, who will most likely discontinue the drug immediately. The same is true if fever, swelling, breathing problems, or other complications develop. Studies find that people experiencing such problems recover completely after stopping the medication.

Between two and five out of ten people do not respond to the first antidepressant they are given; Prozac is no exception. This doesn't mean these people should not be given the drug, but it does mean they should be switched if it is found to be ineffective after a four-to-six-week trial.

Of course, people should not take any medication if they don't need it. People who are not experiencing depression, or one of the other illnesses thought to respond to the drug, have no use for Prozac. It is not a recreational drug; it does not lift the mood of a normal person, nor does it provide a "high" or alter one's consciousness. It is a powerful medication with a specific application and should not be taken by people who are not ill.

HOW MUCH PROZAC SHOULD PEOPLE TAKE?

The key to successful pharmacologic treatment is giving the right drug to the right people in the right amounts. Compared to other antidepressants, Prozac is relatively easy for physicians to prescribe and for patients to use.

Prozac comes in green-and-white capsules each containing a 20-milligram (mg) dose of fluoxetine. Clinical trials on over 10,000 patients before the drug was approved, plus the experience of millions of patients since Prozac hit the market, indicate that people with depression who respond to Prozac usually do just fine taking one 20-mg capsule a day. That's not always the case. Some people may need daily doses of 40 or perhaps even 60 mg. In rare cases, people have used 80 mg or more a day.

Even in the higher doses, Prozac can often be taken just once a day. This is a decided advantage over other antidepressants that must be taken two, three, even four times a day. The easier a drug is to use, the easier it is for people to comply with the regimen and the better the chance that they'll improve. (There is some evidence that certain patients may do well by taking 80 mg of Prozac no more than *once a week*.)

One common misconception people have concerning medicine is the idea that "if some is good, more must be better." Studies have shown this is not true with Prozac. Higher doses do not necessarily result in more antidepressant effect. Somewhat surprisingly, in many cases, a dose of 20 mg actually does a better job than two or three times that amount. What's more, the lower the dose, the lower the risk of unwanted side effects. Symptoms of Prozac overdose include agitation and restlessness.

Most patients take their daily Prozac capsule in the morning. There are exceptions. If people experience nausea, it may be better for them to take their medicine at mealtime. Research has shown that the effectiveness of Prozac, unlike some other drugs, is not affected by the presence of food in the stomach.

Another exception to the morning-dose routine might arise if a patient is having trouble sleeping. Prozac can be a little stimulating; while that can be desirable when depression slows you down, some people find it unpleasant. Prozac's long half-life also means that it can take a while for each dose to "kick in." Thus people who take their capsules in the morning may feel a little revved up just when it's time to hit the hay. The solution is simple: Take the medicine in the middle of the day, so that twelve hours later, while the Prozac is peaking, the patient is sleeping.

One advantage that the tricyclic antidepressants (TCAs) have is that we can monitor a patient's blood and see how much of the drug has entered the bloodstream. This information is useful because it helps us figure out how an individual patient is responding to treatment and what to do about it. To take a hypothetical example, if Patient A isn't getting better with 50 units of Drug X in his system, we can raise the dose and monitor the blood until we reach 75 units and see if that works. Conversely, Patient B might experience severe side effects with 50 units of Drug X; we might then lower the dose to 25 units and see if that makes a difference. Blood monitoring makes this fine-tuning possible.

We don't yet have the technology to monitor blood levels of Prozac, which is a drawback. Prozac, however, is relatively easy to use. Most patients who take it get better using fairly predictable doses and without experiencing severe side effects. When blood tests are developed, doctors will be able to tailor doses even more precisely, which should help increase the drug's success rate.

If Prozac doesn't seem to work for a patient, there are many options. One is to switch to another type of antidepressant drug entirely. Another possibility, though, is to give Prozac a little while longer to see what happens. As with all antidepressants, there is a delay before the effects of Prozac appear. Usually the delay is about three weeks, but it can be longer.

Recently I prescribed Prozac for a patient; after a

month he complained that nothing was happening. I stopped the Prozac and switched him to another drug. Within a week—a suspiciously short time—he was feeling better. Two weeks later, though, he felt much worse. Looking back, I realized I had taken him off Prozac just as it was about to start working. He hadn't been taking the new drug long enough for me to believe it was responsible for his improvement. Two weeks after the switch the patient was clearly experiencing an unpleasant interaction between the two drugs that were now competing within his body. I put him back on Prozac alone, and he has done fine ever since. The point is, this particular patient needed perhaps five weeks of Prozac therapy, rather than the usual three or four, before he noticed signs of improvement.

In a few cases, though, a combination of two antidepressants can be, if you'll excuse the expression, just what the doctor ordered. For example, a combination of Prozac and a more sedating drug like trazodone (sold under the name Desyrel) might be good for people who have trouble sleeping.

Many patients are concerned that, once they are placed on an antidepressant, they will have to keep taking it forever. In a few cases that may be true. As a rule, though, I will ask a patient to keep using the medication for at least six months after the symptoms subside. If the coast seems clear, I will suggest that the person then stop taking the drug while we watch for any recurring signs of trouble. Fortunately, given the way Prozac works in the body, there is little chance that people will experience any withdrawal symptoms when they stop taking it, because *it takes three or four weeks for the drug to leave the system completely.* Thus the shift to a drug-free state involves not a sudden "cold turkey" withdrawal but is a smooth, gradual transition.

IS PROZAC EFFECTIVE?

Drug makers don't usually spend millions of dollars and years of research to put a drug on the market if it offers no clear advantages over other products. It's safe to assume that any drug that makes it through the FDA approval process is effective.

The more important question is whether Prozac is *more* effective for depression than other available drugs. The answer—a somewhat surprising one, given all the recent hoopla—is no. (However, Prozac may be more effective than other medications for other conditions such as obsessive-compulsive disorder, as we'll see in the next chapter.) Studies show that, depending on how skillful they are, doctors can expect that between 60 percent and 80 percent of their depressed patients will improve once they've found the right medication for a particular patient. The success rate with Prozac is pretty much the same.

An important factor in how effective a drug will be is how likely the patient is to comply with the treatment. Because Prozac is so easy to use and produces so few severe side effects, compliance is less of a problem. The more willing patients are to take their medicine, the greater the chance they'll get better.

How does Prozac stack up against other drugs in relieving depression? For that matter, is Prozac better than using no drugs at all?

One study reported that, after five weeks of use, people taking either Prozac or the tricyclic drug imipramine were no better off than those taking a placebo (a pill containing no active ingredients). A week later, however, a clear difference emerged. While 10 percent of those taking the placebo and 56 percent of those on imipramine were rated as improved, 65 percent of those taking Prozac were significantly better. Other studies found Prozac and imipramine roughly comparable in efficacy, but gave higher marks to Prozac because it produced fewer side effects and because fewer patients dropped out of treatment than did those taking imipramine.

Other studies comparing Prozac and the tricyclic

amitriptyline found that both drugs worked equally well. Actually, depressed patients whose symptoms include high levels of anxiety or physical complaints such as headache may do better on amitriptyline or nortriptyline. Amitriptyline can cause sedation; it's possible (but not too likely) that some people taking the drug interpret this effect as helping relieve their depression.

A study comparing Prozac with amitriptyline and doxepin, another antidepressant, in older patients found that all of these drugs relieve depression to about the same degree. Prozac had fewer overall side effects, but the other drugs seemed to work better for patients with sleep disturbance and anxiety.

An antidepressant called mianserin is used in Europe and the United Kingdom and may soon be approved for use in this country. One study found no difference in effectiveness between mianserin and Prozac. However, there was one key distinction: Patients reported significantly *fewer* suicidal thoughts with Prozac than they did with the other drug. This is an important finding, given the current concern about Prozac and suicide, which is discussed in Chapter 6.

SIDE EFFECTS

Studies show that Prozac is basically on a par with other drugs in its overall ability to relieve depression. If that's true, is there a reason for doctors to choose Prozac over the other tried-and-true medications?

Yes there is, and it's a compelling reason, too. Prozac causes fewer troublesome side effects.

Based on more than one thousand "patient-years" of worldwide experience with the drug, data shows Prozac is a lot easier on most patients than other antidepressants. In fact, a number of the patients treated with Prozac have expressed doubts they were even taking a "real drug" at all.

Of course, every drug can cause unwanted reactions.

SIDE EFFECTS OF PROZAC

- Most common (approximate rate):
  Nausea (21%)
  Headache (20%)
  Insomnia (14%)
  Diarrhea (12%)
  Drowsiness (12%)
- Other side effects:
  Anxiety (10%)
  Dry mouth (10%)
  Loss of appetite (9%)
  Tremor (8%)
  Upper respiratory infection (7%)
  Dizziness (6%)
- Infrequent effects (less than 5%):
  Fatigue
  Constipation
  Abdominal pain
  Flu-like syndrome
  Visual disturbance
  Nasal congestion
  Sinus infection
  Cough
  Sexual dysfunction
  Mania

(For that matter, even psychoanalysis or other forms of intense psychotherapy can produce side effects. These effects may include economic hardship, anxiety, interfering with work or personal time, and a kind of "addiction" to the therapy itself.) The tricyclics are notorious for causing dry mouth, irritability, constipation, and weight gain. Generally, the side effects associated with Prozac are less severe, easier to tolerate, and more likely to disappear within a week or so after they start. In fact, in some studies, the rate of side effects was found to be about the same as that seen in people given a placebo. As a rule, 15 percent of patients stop taking the medication due to adverse effects. Often we can control the effects simply by cutting down on the dosage.

Nausea

The problem that people undergoing Prozac therapy are most likely to encounter is persistent nausea. A short while after taking their daily dose of Prozac, some people feel they may vomit (although they rarely do). Usually this feeling passes in two or three hours. If it persists, it may help the patient to take Prozac with a meal, or to take only half a dose at a time. Occasionally, though, the nausea doesn't subside and may even get worse, becoming so unpleasant that people who can't put up with it stop taking the drug entirely.

Headache

At first glance, a 20-percent incidence of headache following Prozac seems high. However, placebos also "caused" headache in up to 15 percent of people in these studies, which makes it harder to know if such adverse events are directly due to the Prozac.

Insomnia

Prozac can be stimulating, causing sleep disturbance in from 5 to 15 percent of patients. This side effect, like many others, is apparently related to the drug's impact on serotonin, one of the neurotransmitters involved in regulating the sleep-wake cycle. However, only about 2 percent of people experiencing insomnia think the problem is bad enough to give up the medicine. A similar percentage of people experience drowsiness troublesome enough to cause them to abandon their use of Prozac. Patients who experience disturbed sleep might try taking their medicine later in the day or try a combination of Prozac and another antidepressant such as trazodone, which can be sedating.

Anxiety

This jittery, restless feeling resembling a super caffeine "buzz" may crop up in one out of ten patients within the first few days after they begin taking Prozac. Anxiety can be a symptom of depression; for some people, Prozac triggers or worsens the problem. One patient complained she was so uncomfortably edgy that she felt like peeling off her skin and rolling in the snow to cool down. Next to nausea, anxiety is the second most common reason patients give for stopping with Prozac.

Mania

Mania is a mood marked by excessive elation, hyperactivity, agitation, and accelerated thinking and speaking. Some reports find that perhaps 1 percent of people taking Prozac may experience a period of mania or near mania. This rate compares favorably to that seen in patients using TCA's and MAOI's. In cases of Prozac-related mania, the problem is easily managed by cutting back on the drug, by carefully administering lithium along with the Prozac, or, if necessary, by stopping it completely.

Sexual Dysfunction

Although not a frequent occurrence, some people, especially men, notice sexual problems while taking Prozac. In some cases this may mean difficulty getting an erection, trouble reaching orgasm, or a problem with ejaculation. However, the incidence of such problems can be even higher with the tricyclics. One report told of four women and one man on Prozac unable to achieve orgasm through any form of sexual stimulation. Even so, only one of these people wanted to stop taking the drug!

Other Reactions

Reports occasionally appear in the medical literature of a patient or two experiencing a unique reaction to Prozac.

In one report, a woman suddenly noticed that shortly after taking Prozac she began yawning—and then during the next two hours experienced twenty-four orgasms, which she rated in intensity as one to five on a scale of ten. Another notes that a woman with multiple sclerosis found her MS symptoms got worse while she was on Prozac. Two patients developed eye twitches. A few people with severe disorders such as schizophrenia or borderline personality disorder became extremely slow or even catatonic after taking Prozac along with certain other drugs.

Such reports remind us that, while we need all the information we can get about the drugs we use, one or two such cases hardly establish a trend. These reports may do nothing more than document coincidences that are not related to the use of medication at all. The only way we can know for certain whether a drug poses a serious risk is to obtain a lot of data from properly designed studies involving large numbers of people.

In Chapter 6 I'll discuss the thorny issue of whether Prozac can trigger suicide or violent behavior. For now let me say that the evidence it does so is pretty weak, while the evidence is convincing that Prozac actually *prevents* suicide by relieving depression and returning a sense of hope to people.

POSSIBLE ADVANTAGES OF PROZAC

Recent research shows that, in addition to its safety and efficacy, there may be other reasons that favor the use of Prozac in depression. Some of these reasons are well supported by evidence; others are much more speculative.

Weight Loss

Ever since the first antidepressants came on the scene, patients have complained that these drugs caused them to gain weight. Putting on pounds is a real problem for people who, because of their depression, are already struggling with low self-esteem. Part of the excitement surrounding Prozac was stirred up by some strong evidence that *this drug, unlike the tricyclics, is less likely to promote weight gain.*

Read that last sentence again carefully. It does not say that Prozac necessarily *causes* weight loss, but that it does *not always lead to weight gain.* The difference is subtle, but important.

The weight-related effects of Prozac are apparently connected to the drug's impact on the serotonin system. As we've seen, Prozac enhances the neurotransmitter's ability to carry its messages, one of which is to tell the brain to stop eating. It's possible, too, that the weight loss is due in part to the nausea that sometimes accompanies use of Prozac. Also, because many people with depression get less sleep, they may be burning more calories over the course of a day. A lot more research is needed to pinpoint the facts in these circumstances.

Unfortunately, when reports began to appear associating Prozac with weight loss, many people jumped to the conclusion that Prozac might work as a diet pill. Who knows, they thought, it may even be a cure for obesity! A cold, hard look at the facts, however, suggests a somewhat different picture.

In one study, for example, a group of people taking Prozac shed an average of nearly four pounds each in six weeks. In comparison, a group taking amitriptyline gained nearly five pounds in the same period, a difference that, in statistical terms, is highly significant. Another study found that patients taking Prozac lost roughly a pound and a half, while those taking mianserin gained close to four pounds. Two studies found that obese individuals who were not depressed and who took Prozac lost an average of close to ten pounds in eight weeks. Other researchers report similar findings. These figures are averages, which means most people's weight changed more or less than the number given.

Some people read these studies and think, "Hey, great—Prozac makes you lose ten pounds in eight weeks!" Grabbing their calculators, they come to the conclusion that they could lose sixty-five pounds in a year!

The truth is, not everybody taking Prozac does lose weight. Some actually gain a little. One study, for example, reported that 65 percent of people taking Prozac (and 20 percent of those taking imipramine) for six weeks dropped an average of about a pound. Conversely, 65 percent of those on imipramine gained close to two pounds—but so did 25 percent of those taking Prozac. What's more, some researchers note that the heaviest people experienced the most weight loss; people who were underweight actually tended to gain weight. On the surface, that seems like good news: Fat people lose weight, skinny people gain it. Interpreted another way, though, it means that people who are only somewhat above their desired weight may not notice any change at all.

I have given Prozac to a number of people who had anorexia as well as depression. These patients did very well on the medication. Not only did their moods lift, they also gained a little weight. In these patients, Prozac did not prevent weight gain from taking place.

One other point: Weight-loss studies so far have followed patients for just a few weeks. It might be that Prozac users lose some pounds in the early stage of treatment, but see the loss taper off and eventually stop.

In other words, ten pounds in eight weeks will probably not translate into sixty-five pounds a year. Again, scientists have a lot more homework to do before we know what role, if any, Prozac will play in weight loss.

Less Sedation

Another advantage of Prozac is that it does not generally cause sedation, as can some of the tricyclics. When a person experiences agitation as a symptom of depression, a little sedation can sometimes be a desirable thing. But if people don't need to be calmed down, then Prozac may be the better choice.

Does Not Cause a "High"

Some people think feelings of anxiety or jitteriness means Prozac is giving them a "high." Not true. Usually the drug simply returns people to their normal good mood, not an artificially elevated one. *It has no effect on people whose moods are just fine to begin with.* (In Italy, people can buy Prozac illegally on the street, where it is known as "Bye-Bye Blues." Sorry, bambini. If you aren't clinically depressed, you're probably throwing your hardearned *lire* away in search of a buzz that isn't there.)

Less Toxic

Depression can produce suicidal thinking. Tragically, prescribing highly toxic drugs to heal depression may be putting a weapon of self-destruction into a vulnerable person's hands. The tricyclics cause nearly forty deaths for every million prescriptions. Statistics from the United Kingdom show that three out of every hundred people who overdose on tricyclics die as a result.

Prozac overdose, however, is not likely to be lethal. Before Prozac came on the market here, there were reports in the medical literature of thirty-eight cases of overdose with the drug. Two of those cases resulted in death; *neither death occurred in a person taking Prozac by itself.* Both victims, in other words, had used at least one other drug at the same time. People who do overdose on Prozac, whether on purpose or by accident, seem to suffer relatively minor effects, including nausea, vomiting, tremor, and high agitation.

Many studies have noted that, of the antidepressants available today, Prozac poses the lowest risk of side effects related to the heart and thus may be preferable for patients with heart conditions. While rapid heartbeat, faulty heart rhythms, changes in blood pressure, or related problems are common with other antidepressants, they occur in less than 1 percent of patients using Prozac. Similarly, unlike the tricyclics and the MAOI's, Prozac does not increase the risk of seizure, even in high doses.

Not Addicting

Prozac is not known to be addicting, especially compared to amphetamines and other appetite-suppressing drugs. Some people might think they never want to stop taking the medication, since they feel so much better after their depression has lifted. This is not the same thing as addiction, however; it is the normal response of someone whose life has dramatically improved. An addict is someone who develops both a psychological and a physiological dependence on a substance for which their body has no real need. Addicts become compulsive in their behavior involving the substance, and depend on it to get them through the day. They develop tolerance—that is, they need higher and higher doses to achieve the same effect. When they do stop, they experience symptoms of withdrawal. This simply doesn't happen with Prozac. For example, people who respond to this medication don't feel they have to keep taking higher doses.

No Withdrawal Syndrome

What's more, there is no withdrawal syndrome once the drug has been stopped. Typically a patient keeps taking the medication for perhaps six months to a year after the symptoms have abated. At that time doctors often suggest that the patient try going without Prozac to see what happens. (It's best if the medication is continued until some potential crisis, such as final exams, year-end sales conferences, or a move to a different part of the country has passed.) The doctor will review the symptoms of depression and instruct the patient to watch for signs that the problem is recurring. Because of Prozac's long half-life, it is possible to stop taking the medicine "cold turkey" without risking any physical complications or a sudden recurrence of depression.

It may be better, however, to taper off the medication somewhat gradually, perhaps by taking one capsule every other day for a week, then stopping altogether. Occasionally patients who are reducing their dosage may feel a sense of anxiety about suffering a relapse. The physician will stay in touch with the patient to make sure that these symptoms don't get worse. Sometimes, however, patients do notice some of the classic depressive symptoms: changes in appetite or sleep, loss of energy, low mood. Remember, though, these are signs of *relapse*, not of withdrawal. If these symptoms appear, the patient should visit the physician, who may then decide to start the medication again. If Prozac was effective before, it will usually be effective in treating the relapse.

Less Mental and Physical Impairment

In one study, researchers gauged the effects of antidepressants on the ability to drive a car. A battery of tests measured agility, coordination, and reflexes. People taking Prozac did much better than those using tricyclics or alcohol—or both. Even when people took Prozac and alcohol, they experienced no significant reduction in their ability to function. Such findings may provide the tiniest of hints that for some people Prozac may offset the effects of alcohol by improving eye coordination and reaction time. We'll need to see a lot more hard data, however, before we can accept such findings as fact. Meanwhile people taking Prozac should be very careful about driving a car until they are sure the drug does not affect their alertness.

INTERACTIONS BETWEEN PROZAC AND OTHER DRUGS

Most medicines are extremely powerful. When you put two or more drugs into one person's body the results can be surprising, not to mention dangerous. Drugs can interact in several ways. They can cancel each other out. Even worse, one drug may make the other become even stronger, producing overreaction or serious side effects. Signs of drug interactions, however, do not always mean that therapy has to be stopped completely. It can simply mean that we need to watch the patient more carefully or adjust the timing or quantity of the dose.

Your physician and pharmacist keep careful records of every drug you are taking. You should know in advance if there's a chance two drugs will get into a "turf war." For example, Prozac can increase the supply of the heart drug digitalis or the anticoagulant warfarin in the bloodstream. That means more of the drug circulates freely— more than the patient's body may be able to handle. By monitoring a patient's blood, we can usually spot signs of trouble and make the necessary adjustments.

Tricyclic Antidepressants

Prozac can enhance the effects of the tricyclics and cause such problems as insomnia, loss of appetite, and anxiety. Tricyclics already pose a risk to the heart and may provoke seizures; when used in combination with

POSSIBLE INTERACTIONS WITH PROZAC

NOTE: The literature contains reports showing that Prozac may interact with the following specific drugs. It is reasonable to assume that similar interactions may also occur with other drugs in the same categories.

Tricyclic antidepressants
    Norpramine (desipraminc)
    Pamelor (nortriptyline)
    Sinequan (doxepin)
    Tofranil (imipramine)
Monoamine oxidase inhibitors
    Nardil (phenelzine sulfate)
    Parmate (tranylcypromine)
Other antidepressants
    Desyrel (trazodone)
Antianxiety medications
    Valium (diazepam)
    Xanax (alprazolam)
Other drugs
    anticoagulants
    digoxin
    lithium
    tryptophan

DRUGS NOT FOUND TO INTERFERE SIGNIFICANTLY WITH PROZAC

    analgesics
    antacids
    antibiotics
    antihistamines
    blood pressure medications (beta blockers)
    diuretics
    oral contraceptives
    thyroid hormones
    ulcer medication (Tagamet)

Prozac, the risk is even higher. However, it's not usually necessary for people to take two antidepressants at the same time, so the problem is easily avoided.

MAOI's

The MAOI's pose a different challenge. As we've already noted, Prozac's long half-life means that fluoxetine molecules remain in the body for up to a month. When Prozac and an MAOI mix, trouble can arise. There have been at least three reports of people who died after taking these two drugs, although we have no proof that the deaths are drug–related. Nevertheless, the patient should wait at least five weeks between the last dose of Prozac and the first dose of an MAOI, or two weeks after stopping an MAOI and starting with Prozac.

Anxiety Drugs

A few studies note that Prozac can slow down the rate at which the body breaks down the antianxiety drug diazepam (sold under the brand name Valium). Anxiety is common in depression, and many people take Valium as part of their treatment, so any potential interaction between it and an antidepressant is of concern. However, even though Prozac tends to make Valium remain in the bloodstream a little longer, this change doesn't seem to translate into any serious clinical problems. It's possible the same is true of other antianxiety drugs in the same group, but I haven't seen any reports that address the question.

Lithium

A number of reports find that Prozac can interfere with lithium's ability to control manic attacks. On the other hand, the combination of Prozac and lithium also appears to help some depressed people who don't get better on either drug alone. As we gain more experience, we'll learn which people are good candidates for this combination and which should avoid it.

The point of this chapter has been to show you how Prozac looks to someone who must decide whether or not it might help a person suffering from depression. You've learned what happens to the drug inside the body, and also which people are most likely to benefit from Prozac and how they should use it. For both physician and patients, the main concerns are effectiveness and safety. While Prozac works about as well as most other antidepressants, it has a better track record in terms of side effects, and has other advantages as well. Prozac can interfere with certain other drugs, but overall it is a very good choice for many people trapped by the gloom and despair of their terrible illness.

The focus of discussion so far has been on the use of Prozac in the treatment of depression, since that is the only disorder for which this drug is officially approved. However, clinical research is generating a growing mountain of evidence that Prozac may be useful in a number of other conditions as well, as we'll see in the next chapter. Prozac doesn't yet have the formal blessing of the FDA for these "off-label" uses. Nonetheless, support is swelling among two important constituencies: One is doctors; the other is the patients under their care, for whom Prozac offers hope that their suffering may one day end.

BEYOND DEPRESSION:
OTHER USES
FOR PROZAC

When the serotonin system misfires, a lot of things can go wrong. Because serotonin affects mood, some people become depressed. Because it is involved in regulating eating, some develop eating disorders. Others develop other problems ranging from obsessive-compulsive disorder to alcoholism. Depression can be present in any of these problems. It didn't take long after the arrival of Prozac for some doctors to realize that the drug might be useful in other serotonin-related disorders.

That intuition is proving correct. As these reports trickle in, interest in this medication mounts.

EATING DISORDERS

There are two main types of eating disorders: anorexia nervosa and bulimia. Both affect women predominantly.

Many eating-disordered women come from families

where the incidence of depression, alcoholism, substance abuse, or other psychiatric disorders is higher than average. Social or psychological pressures may also contribute to the onset or severity of a disorder, or to its particular pattern of symptoms, but the main source of the problem is a neurochemical malfunction.

Anorexia

Victims of anorexia (the word means "without appetite") starve themselves until they have lost at least 15 percent of their body weight. They become fixated on the goal of becoming as thin as possible, thinner than anyone has ever been. Their illness causes them to have an overwhelming fear of being fat; they develop such a distorted image of what their bodies look like that they claim to have "huge thighs" or "pot bellies" even though to an objective observer they are as skinny as skeletons. Many anorexics develop bizarre eating habits or beliefs about food. One patient, for example, ate nothing all day but a "sandwich" made of lettuce leaves and mustard. Perhaps 95 percent of people with anorexia are women; an estimated one out of a hundred (some experts say one in eight hundred) adolescent girls may be anorexic.

If self-starvation doesn't cause them to lose weight fast enough, many anorexics will take other drastic steps. They may abuse laxatives or diuretics to rid themselves of food faster and may burn off even more calories through compulsive exercise. If anorexia isn't treated, its victims can—and do—starve to death.

The human body, however, doesn't usually take such threats lying down. The urge to eat—and thus survive—is extraordinarily strong. When a starving person succumbs to the urge to eat, she often does so by going on a binge. After the binge the person often feels an overwhelming need to get rid of the food she has eaten. She does so through self-induced vomiting. When this pattern begins she has crossed the boundary into another category of eating disorder. She has become a bulimic anorexic.

Bulimia

The term *bulimia* is derived from Greek words meaning "ox hunger." The main symptom of bulimia is a pattern of binge-eating. In a short time a binger can put down an astounding amount of food: whole packages of cookies, quarts of ice cream, bags of chips, burgers, fries, entire pizzas, you name it. Many, but not all, bulimics also induce vomiting to purge themselves of their meal. Some people with bulimia start off as anorexics, but more often bulimia arises as a disorder in its own right. Bulimia also affects primarily women. As many as 4 to 14 percent of college-age women may be bulimic to some extent.

Treating Eating Disorders with Prozac

For several years I was the head of the eating disorders unit at a psychiatric hospital in New Jersey. In dealing with hundreds of patients, I saw first-hand the suffering and devastation that these conditions can cause. As you might imagine, I was very interested in any form of treatment that could help these women get their lives back to normal as quickly as possible.

I carefully followed the developments related to the use of fluoxetine (the active ingredient in Prozac) both before and after it reached the market. I had seen reports that fluoxetine caused rats to eat less, even though the animals had been deprived of food for most of a day and were given food they normally liked to eat. Such results suggested that fluoxetine might work to control appetite. The drug might thus be useful both for weight control and for the treatment of eating disorders.

My impression is that Prozac is indeed very helpful in these areas, but not necessarily because it suppresses appetite. Prozac probably works because it corrects an underlying serotonin malfunction and thus alleviates faulty eating behavior. Other antidepressants that don't affect appetite can also work in eating disorders because they, too, manipulate the serotonin system.

My colleagues and I tested the idea that fluoxetine could contribute to weight loss by giving the medication to two groups of bulimic women. One group included five women who were at least 10 percent above their ideal weight, while the other group included eleven bulimics whose weight was normal. All five of the overweight patients, and a total of nine out of the sixteen patients, noticed at least a 75 percent reduction in their binging and purging while taking Prozac. As a group, the women lost a little weight, the average loss being about three pounds. Analysis of the data showed this weight loss was *not* due to the decrease in bingeing and purging—that is, it was a direct effect of the drug. We concluded that while Prozac may produce modest weight loss, it can lead to significant improvements in bulimic symptoms.

In one recent year-long study at the University of Pittsburgh, Dr. Marsha D. Marcus and her colleagues assembled some women who were binge eaters and who were also 25 percent above their ideal body weight. They divided them into two groups. Members of one group were given Prozac and were also shown ways to improve their eating habits through diet and behavior. The second group was taught diet and behavior modification and given a placebo.

The results were surprising. The group given Prozac lost significantly more weight than the placebo group— an average of a pound and a half per week, with a total weight loss averaging about thirty pounds. However, this group only lost weight during the first six months; during the rest of the year they *regained* an average of about fifteen pounds. Similar results were seen at another hospital conducting a comparable study at the same time. The researchers concluded that Prozac may lead to weight loss for a limited time, but may not cause further weight loss after a certain point unless patients are given ongoing support and watched closely to make sure they are complying with the drug regimen.

Some doctors giving their bulimic patients antidepressants are concerned about the high dropout rate. In one study, for example, twenty-seven bulimic patients did well taking an MAO inhibitor, but after four months twenty-four of these patients stopped taking the medication because of side effects; nineteen of the twenty-seven relapsed either while taking the drug or after they stopped. Another study found that eleven out of eighteen patients had stopped taking an MAOI within a year after they had started, largely because of side effects. Compliance was obviously a problem for these patients. Remember, however, that such results may be skewed by the "center effect" mentioned in Chapter 2: If the researchers at a treatment center aren't fully committed to the use of medications, they may not encourage patients to stay with the prescription or may not be interested in finding ways to manage side effects should they occur.

In another study, researchers found medications could keep up to 65 percent of their patients free of bulimic symptoms. Doing so, however, meant working harder to find the *right* drug for each patient. These researchers tried their patients on as many as four medications, one at a time, before hitting on the right one. In this study, out of the seventeen patients who continued taking their medication and whose bulimia had completely remitted, six were taking Prozac (one was taking Prozac and lithium).

As a result of these studies, and from my own experience, I often consider Prozac my first choice of treatment for bulimics, along with supportive psychotherapy and nutritional counseling. Though Prozac may help relieve bulimic symptoms and reduce weight, many patients may need to try several drugs before finding the one that's best for them. Prozac is a reasonable choice for these patients, not just because it often works, but because it leads to fewer complications with side effects. In addition, however, patients may need other kinds of support to help them put an end to the chaos their disorder has brought to their lives.

Prozac in the Treatment of Anorexia

Anorexia is a different problem. Obviously people who refuse to eat don't need to be taking a medication that may reduce their appetite and cause them to lose weight.

Many anorexics already abuse laxatives and diuretics. It's reasonable to be concerned that a woman whose goal is to become "the thinnest person in the world" might also abuse a drug she has heard will help her control her eating. A doctor reported recently on a woman with anorexia and depression who took part in a Prozac study. (She didn't bother telling the researchers about her eating disorder.) She noticed her appetite decreased after ten days on Prozac. Although her depression didn't lift, she told the researchers it did so they would keep giving her the medication. This single case report proves nothing, but it does show that it's possible some people may use a good drug for the wrong reasons.

However, as we have seen, some studies suggest that while Prozac may reduce weight in people who need to lose weight, it doesn't necessarily do so in people whose weight is about where it should be.

I have cautiously given Prozac to dozens of anorexic patients with depression, whom I've then watched very carefully. I also put these patients on a course of psychotherapy and make sure they receive nutritional counseling. In many cases I have seen good results with this three-pronged treatment strategy. The medication fixes the fundamental biological problem that is disrupting their eating; the psychotherapy helps them feel better about themselves; and the diet counseling teaches them how to eat again in healthier ways.

One tantalizing case was reported a few years ago by a leading eating disorders expert, Dr. James M. Ferguson. A woman who had been starving herself for more than twenty-five years had begun cycling between periods of starvation and episodes of bingeing and purging. Her doctors had tried the whole gamut of medications—tricyclics, MAOI's, even antipsychotics. Either these products did her no good or she suffered severe adverse reactions, including fever and seizures. She was given fluoxetine; after two weeks she was taking 80 mg a day without serious side effects. Within another week she was totally free of bulimic symptoms and her mood had improved dramatically. Even more surprising, she had actually gained six pounds—*without* any changes in her diet or eating habits (except that she began eating a wider variety of foods) and *without* any other form of psychotherapy.

As encouraging as these reports are, we still need good studies with many patients to show whether Prozac is most likely to help anorexics, bulimics, or, as in the case just cited, those who have symptoms of both anorexia and bulimia.

Obesity

With plenty of palatable food available, with people eating better and taking better care of themselves, the average human height and weight is increasing. Nonetheless, it's an unfortunate fact of life in our society that "thin is in." Researchers have found that, over the last two decades or so, the measurements of those "ideal" images of feminine beauty—the women in *Playboy* centerfolds and those chosen to be Miss America—have become smaller. *Today these beauty queens are thinner than 95 percent of the women in this country!* That's a pretty tough standard for the average woman to compete with. Nonetheless, many women try.

Recently scientists have found evidence that the human body is born with a built-in genetic program that determines our ideal weight. You may have heard this referred to as the "set-point theory." Circumstances being right, the body will reach its set-point weight and then fight to maintain that weight within a certain range. The set-point concept helps explain why many people find it difficult if not impossible to lose weight and keep it off. Their bodies may be struggling to return their weight to its preprogrammed level. Thus trying to lower the body's weight may be as hopeless a quest as trying to lower one's normal temperature from 98.6 to 95 degrees Fahrenheit.

However, a recent study on obese women offers some hope. In this study, conducted by Dr. Benjamin Levy in Hartford, Connecticut, women were given Prozac and also placed on a balanced, 1200-calorie-a-day diet and encouraged to exercise. This combination of strategies produced some encouraging results. Over the course of a year, for example, one woman lost sixty pounds and noticed that she no longer experienced the constant craving for junk food that had led to her weight gain in the first place.

It may be that in this study, the weight loss due to use of the medication resulted at least in part from improved mood and higher self-esteem, which in turn helped the patients work harder to follow their diet and exercise program. In any case, more research is needed before we can state with certainty that Prozac is an appropriate medication for the treatment of obesity.

OBSESSIVE-COMPULSIVE DISORDER (OCD)

- Joan D., thirty-six years old, could not leave her house without checking each door and window exactly four times to make sure it was locked. She often became so concerned about whether she might have forgotten to lock one of her doors that she had to leave work and race home to check the house again.

- Mark W., eighteen, was extraordinarily fearful of germs. He took two-hour-long showers every morning, not minding that he ran out of hot water after about twenty minutes. He washed his hands perhaps fifty times a day, and placed each item of laundry in a plastic Zip-Loc bag as he pulled it from the dryer to keep it "sterile."
- Pat C., twenty, couldn't get through the day without completing a complicated series of rituals. She had to eat every crumb of food on her plate. She had to read every word of the morning newspaper, including the want ads. She clipped every coupon, whether or not she ever used the products the coupons were for. She had to brush her hair a certain number of times, lace her shoes so that the ends came out precisely even, and so on and on and on . . .

Obsessive-compulsive disorder (OCD) made the headlines recently when a survey found that perhaps as many as twenty-five out of every thousand people in this country suffer from its symptoms—three times as many as suffer from schizophrenia. Perhaps 70 percent of people with OCD develop the condition between the ages of ten and twenty-three. The French refer to OCD by the poetic name of *folie de doute*—the doubting disease. As the above anecdotes show, people with OCD experience crippling doubts that things will be well unless they behave in a certain way.

Obsessions are recurrent persistent ideas or thoughts that intrude on a person's mind. A person may attempt to ignore or suppress these thoughts or "cancel" them through some kind of action. People with OCD are not suffering from delusions—they know these thoughts come from inside themselves and are not the result of "voices" or hallucinations, as in psychosis. Typical obsessions include a disgusted response to body waste, concern about dirt or disease such as cancer or AIDS, fear of toxic chemicals, fear of losing things, a need for symmetry, or a need to count, check, speak all thoughts that pop into the head, or apologize constantly.

Compulsions are repetitive behaviors performed as a response to an obsession and carried out in a rigid, stereotyped way that consumes at least an hour of the person's day. There is a clear connection between the obsession (germs, for example) and the compulsion (excessive washing). People with OCD know their behavior is unreasonable and are distressed about what is happening to them. They often can't carry out any kind of normal routine and have trouble functioning at home, on the job, or in society. Commonly seen compulsions include cleaning or washing rituals, avoidance of people or things, behavior designed to elicit reassurance about health, hoarding, arranging, making repetitious statements, and constant counting or checking.

As many as one out of three OCD patients becomes depressed as a result of the disorder. Many other patients, however, experience depression first. Extreme feelings of guilt, self-doubt, low self-esteem, or suicidal thinking are typical symptoms of depression; left untreated, these can so overwhelm a person's thinking that they can lead to OCD as a secondary problem. It's also possible for people with OCD to have a personality disorder, such as avoidant or dependent personality disorder, at the same time. Some researchers believe that people with OCD are also at high risk of developing schizophrenia.

Recently an advanced diagnostic technique known as positron emission tomography (PET) scanning has revealed that people with OCD have physical abnormalities in certain parts of their brains. This suggests that people are either born with these abnormalities or they may inherit the tendency to develop such problems later in life. One very strange case a couple of years ago involved an eighteen-year-old Canadian man whose life was being destroyed by his compulsion to wash his hands constantly. Unable to bear his suffering any longer, he attempted suicide by firing a bullet through his head. Amazingly, he survived—and his compulsions disappeared! While I obviously don't recommend this form of self-administered therapy, this anecdote nonetheless supports the notion that OCD arises from a defect in the brain's structure.

The first medication for the treatment of OCD was approved recently by the FDA. This drug, clomipramine (sold under the name Anafranil), is classified as a tricyclic antidepressant. Unlike other tricyclics, however, it seems to work primarily on the serotonin system. Naturally, success with clomipramine led researchers to pursue their intuition that other serotonin uptake inhibitors might have the same effect. So far the results have been encouraging.

In published reports, Prozac helped between 50 and 70 percent of patients with OCD. Studies in France reported improvement in up to 80 percent of OCD patients treated with fluoxetine. Such results are about the same as those seen with clomipramine.

It can take a long time—up to ten weeks—for the effects of these drugs to be noticed. While the standard dose of Prozac in depression is around 20 mg a day, OCD patients have been treated with between 20 and 100 mg a day. Researchers note that OCD patients taking Prozac experience marked reductions in their levels of depression and anxiety, factors which contribute greatly to the general improvement in their well-being. What's more, improvement continued over the five-month period covered in the study, suggesting that long-term treatment may be both necessary and helpful. As usual, the low incidence of side effects with Prozac helped the clinical picture, and helped maintain patient compliance with the treatment.

Some other recent findings: Prozac relieved OCD in

patients whether they were depressed or not. It was also effective in at least one case where the patient was prone to self-multilation. One study found that Prozac helped 80 percent of OCD patients who had obsessive fear of disease, 75 percent of those who were compulsive "checkers," 60 percent of the "hoarders," and 50 percent of those with sexual or aggressive obsessions. Such findings suggest that in the future we may be able to prescribe medications according to the exact patterns of symptoms a patient displays.

As noted earlier, OCD can strike people as young as ten years of age. Prozac may be a good choice of treatment for children, since it has such a low incidence of side effects. In one study, four out of eight children treated with up to 80 mg of Prozac a day found that their washing rituals had virtually disappeared after eight weeks; another two experienced moderate relief. Two other children became agitated and stopped taking the drug. These results compared favorably to those seen with clomipramine.

As with depression, treatment is never as simple as handing the patients their prescriptions and sending them on their way. In my experience, some OCD patients need considerable time or higher than usual doses before they notice any improvement; if, however, ten weeks have passed and things are no better, I will change my strategy. There is a risk that perhaps 20 to 40 percent of OCD patients will relapse within a year after they stop taking Prozac; however, this rate appears to be better than that seen with clomipramine. Some reports raise the concern that OCD patients taking Prozac may be at risk of sexual dysfunction, including loss of libido and inability to reach orgasm.

In some cases patients may respond to a combination of Prozac and another drug. Reports in the literature cite success with combinations that include one of the tricyclics, trazodone, buspirone, or amphetamine. I have also had success using a combination of Prozac and lithium. The antianxiety drugs such as diazepam should probably not be used along with Prozac. Behavior therapy can help, especially when used along with medications.

BODY DYSMORPHIC DISORDER

As mentioned, anorexics often believe that they are "fat" despite their skeletal appearance. In much the same way, some people who are not anorexic may develop a mental disorder that causes them to perceive some part of their body as abnormal in size or appearance. This condition, known as body dysmorphic disorder, usually affects people between adolescence and the age of thirty and can persist for several years if not treated. Some patients with body dysmorphic disorder come from families with a history of affective disorders. People with this problem can usually function fairly well, but they spend inordinate amounts of time looking in the mirror and fretting, and they may avoid coming into contact with other people because they think they are "ugly" or "deformed." While they may actually have a slight abnormality, such people often spend thousands of dollars on useless plastic surgery for a minor or nonexistent problem. While this condition is different than obsessive-compulsive disorder, the two share some features in common.

A report from Dr. Eric Hollander and colleagues at Columbia University in New York tells of one patient with body dysmorphic disorder who felt that the blood vessels in her nose were as obvious as the highways on a Rand-McNally road map. Another believed his cheekbones were hideously distorted. For over eight years, one woman spent up to eight hours a day cutting each hair on her head so that it was perfectly symmetrical. A man in his fifties had four operations to correct his "misshapen" nose, while another man in his twenties was so convinced that his penis was small and ugly that he refused to date or socialize with women and became more and more socially isolated.

The researchers found that these patients generally improved with use of serotonin uptake inhibitors. Clomipramine helped most of these patients, but there was some evidence that Prozac might also be of use. As physicians become more adept at recognizing body dysmorphic disorder, and more skilled in the use of medications to reduce its effects on people's lives, we will learn more about the role of Prozac in managing this strange problem.

ALCOHOLISM

Some exciting preliminary research shows that serotonin uptake inhibitors might work to decrease alcohol intake. In one study, a daily dose of 60 mg of Prozac caused problem drinkers to decrease their alcohol consumption by 17 percent over a two-week period. (Interestingly, there was no difference between Prozac and a placebo when the dose was only 40 mg.) The people in this study also lost an average of around four pounds; this weight loss was found to be due to the medication and not to the reduced alcohol consumption.

Another study found that up to 80 mg of Prozac a day (but not 40 mg) helped ten alcoholics reduce their alcohol consumption by 14 percent during the first week of the study. Intriguingly, this study found that other serotonin uptake inhibitors increased the number of days of abstinence, while Prozac decreased the number of drinks consumed on "drinking days." Both this and the other study found that the doses of Prozac in the treatment of alcoholism needed to be higher than those typically used to manage depression. Behavioral therapy in conjunction with medications helped these patients reduce their drinking even further.

One note: The drop in alcohol consumption in both studies was no more than 17 percent. This may not seem like much, but at least it's a move in the right direction. Future treatment strategies, or newer drugs that also affect serotonin, may one day produce even better results.

Many drugs, including Prozac and alcohol, are broken down by enzymes in the liver. As you are no doubt aware, alcoholism can lead to liver damage known as cirrhosis, in which the liver becomes plugged up like a clogged drain. Up to 8 percent of alcoholics develop cirrhosis—seven times the rate seen among nonalcoholics. People with cirrhosis who take Prozac break down the drug more slowly and have more of the drug in their bloodstream after each dose. They thus may be more sensitive to normal doses of the drug as well as to its potential side effects. I usually cut the dose of Prozac in half if I give it to patients with cirrhosis.

PANIC AND ANXIETY

For the past few years Alison had been virtually unable to leave her house without her husband. She became panicked if she was alone in public, which meant she couldn't go shopping or drive a car by herself, let alone hold down a job. After taking Prozac for three months, however, the symptoms of her disorder, known as agoraphobia, have almost entirely disappeared. "I feel like I'm part of the world again," she says.

Panic attacks are unexpected, recurring feelings that something is horribly wrong. Anxiety is a more chronic, long-term condition. These disorders cause agitation, rapid heartbeat, dizziness, sweating, fear of imminent doom, and so on. Panic and anxiety disorders may turn out to be yet another result of a malfunction in the serotonin system.

Logically, you might assume that antidepressants that produce sedation would be a good choice for people who need to calm down. While that's often true, other antidepressants that *don't* cause sedation can also help relieve panic and anxiety. That's more evidence that these medications provide deep relief by fixing the problem at its source—in the biochemistry of the brain—rather than providing the shallow relief that comes from temporarily relieving one of the symptoms.

We know that between 10 and 20 percent of the time, Prozac can *cause* such side effects as anxiety, tremor, or nervousness. Despite this, as Alison's story shows, Prozac can be effective in treating anxiety disorders, although the doses are usually lower than those needed for depression. One study found that a dose of 5 mg a day (one-fourth the usual dose) reduced anxiety in 80 percent of panic-disorder patients.

Seven out of sixteen patients in another study also became free of panic after using Prozac in doses of up to 5 mg a day. It took about six weeks for panic to subside, while it took about another week for the anxiety to lift. Those who didn't get better, however, tended to report that their anxiety had actually worsened due to the drug. This report also mentions that two of the nine people with panic disorders who didn't respond to Prozac became depressed during the study. These two reported an increase in suicidal thoughts. There's no way to prove whether these thoughts were brought on as a direct result of the medication or whether they were part of the typical pattern of depression symptoms.

Other researchers found that seven out of eight people with panic disorders experienced complete remission of their symptoms using between 10 and 70 mg of Prozac, but eight other patients couldn't tolerate Prozac even at a dose of 10 mg a day. It's possible some of these people might have improved if, as in the other study, the dose had been even lower, although that's not a sure bet.

One anecdotal report mentions a patient who took only 1 mg of Prozac a day and still experienced jitteriness, difficulty concentrating, and an increased incidence of panic attacks. Surprisingly, however, this patient stuck it out; over two weeks his symptoms disappeared. By the end of nearly three months he was taking 10 mg of Prozac at night. He reported that his panic attacks and night terrors had almost disappeared and that his anxiety and obsessive worrying had diminished significantly. Two months later his worrying returned but disappeared again after the patient gradually increased Prozac to 20 mg a night. After three months he continued to do well, reporting that his life had completely changed for the better.

OTHER PROZAC POSSIBILITIES

There is sketchy evidence that Prozac may help in a number of other conditions. As you read the following, keep in mind that we are just beginning to investigate these possibilities. A few anecdotal case reports are not proof; they are nothing more than arrows pointing toward future avenues of research.

Borderline Personality Disorders

If you saw the movie *Fatal Attraction*, you saw a dramatization of what can happen when a person (in this case, the Glenn Close character) suffers from a severe borderline personality disorder. These people—perhaps 2 to 5 percent of the population—experience radical mood swings, have poor self-images, and have very troubled relationships with other people. They may shift from being overly dependent on a person one day to totally rejecting that person the next. They may act impulsively, spending all their money, driving recklessly, indulging in drugs or alcohol or promiscuous sex. They can plunge into and out of intense depression, anxiety, or irritability within the space of a few hours. They often make suicidal gestures or try to mutilate themselves, often in frantic effort to keep from being left alone.

A few years ago I conducted some of the first follow-up research on this complex disorder. My research team observed patients for long periods to see what impact treatment had. These patients had been treated with non-tricyclic antidepressants such as Prozac, antipsychotic medications, psychotherapy, or some combination of these. When we looked at the data, however, we noticed a curious thing: Many of the supposedly borderline patients who also had depression got better after being treated with antidepressants *alone*. Yes, these medications helped because they improved their mood. But improved mood seemed to make their borderline symptoms disappear as well.

It would be logical to assume from these findings that antidepressants relieve borderline personality disorder. We reached a different conclusion, however. We concluded that people who show signs of being borderline are often *misdiagnosed*. What they may actually have is a form of depression. Many borderline patients who are depressed get better on antidepressants or perhaps lithium because their moods lift or stabilize. However, in a large number of cases, depression may be their *only* real illness. They are not really "borderline" at all, and so the only treatment they need is an antidepressant. Prozac may be a good choice in such cases.

Tourette's Syndrome

Tourette's is a disorder probably caused by an inherited brain defect producing muscle tics and strange behavior that resembles obsessive-compulsive disorder. The most notorious symptom of Tourette's is that many of its victims speak uncontrollably, usually in a stream of obscenities. Because Tourette's resembles some forms of OCD, the serotonin uptake inhibitors may work as a form of treatment. In one study a dose of up to 20 mg of Prozac was given to three victims of Tourette's every other day for three months. The severity of their obsessive-compulsive symptoms dropped by one-third. All three patients reported that they were doing better now than they had at any time in the past ten years. The improvement in their muscle and speech tics, however, was less impressive; one patient was significantly better, one worse, and one stayed the same. However, one patient who had symptoms of depression felt much improved after three weeks.

Premenstrual Syndrome

Mood swings and depression can appear as part of PMS. One preliminary report indicates that women with PMS who experience depression may notice improved mood and less severe PMS symptoms after taking Prozac. Researchers are just beginning to explore this area, however, and we need much more data than are currently available.

Nicotine Withdrawal

A preliminary study found that six months after beginning treatment with Prozac, 80 percent of former smokers experienced less irritability and fewer cravings for cigarettes. However, in one of the studies on alcoholism cited earlier, researchers found that while use of 60 mg of Prozac reduced the number of alcoholic drinks consumed, it *increased* the number of cigarettes smoked in a day. Lower doses of Prozac did not prompt this increase. Perhaps in nicotine withdrawal, as in other conditions, response to the drug depends heavily on the exact dosage. It may be, too, that withdrawal from alcohol can stimulate a desire for cigarettes, as many people who quit drinking report. Obviously we need much more research before we can draw any firm conclusions about the use of Prozac as a technique to stop smoking.

Schizophrenia

One study found that symptoms of schizophrenia as well as depression improved in patients who took Prozac in combination with their usual antipsychotic medications. Prozac may have somehow made the other drugs more potent, but it's more likely that Prozac has a direct effect on the brain malfunction that produces schizophrenia, at least in a certain subgroup of people with this disorder. As our work with borderline patients shows, it's always possible, too, that some people thought to be schizophrenic have been misdiagnosed and are actually suffering instead from severe depression.

Exhibitionism

Some people suffer from a OCD-like disorder that compels them to expose themselves to strangers. Usually people with this problem, like those with OCD, are highly distressed by their own behavior. One man who had been an exhibitionist since he was a child tried to hang himself after being arrested. Antipsychotics and tricyclics did no good, but on 40 mg a day of Prozac he gradually noticed that his urge to expose himself abated. Eventually a combination of Prozac and an antipsychotic put a complete end to his exhibitionism for the first time since early childhood.

Dementia

One patient hospitalized after a severe accident was getting out of control. He was having seizures and was agitated, belligerent, and difficult to manage. He couldn't respond to instructions, he chewed holes in his IV lines, he smeared himself with his own feces. Some of the weaker serotonin uptake inhibitors, including trazodone, did nothing. After two weeks on Prozac, however, he calmed down, experiencing no more than one mild outburst a day (compared to eight severe ones before taking the drug). He could now recognize and communicate with the hospital staff, and did not experience sedation, anxiety, or insomnia.

Itchy Skin

A dermatologist treated a patient who for nine years had suffered from aquagenic pruritis, a skin disease marked by tormenting itching. This patient had tried antihistamines, steroids, moisturizers—all to no avail. Not surprisingly, this patient was depressed. Her doctor prescribed Prozac, and almost immediately her itching stopped. Whether this was a result of her improved mood or because of some unknown dermatologic effect, we may never know, but it's an intriguing finding.

PEOPLE AND PROZAC

Paula sat in the chair across from my desk. Her head was down, held there, it seemed, by an invisible hand. Only once during our conversation did her eyes meet mine. I could see her eyes held that strange look of fear, pain, and entrapment common to people gripped by depression. She responded to my questions, but her answers were usually short, more like grunts than words. There were long gaps before she replied, as if she were beaming her answers from someplace beyond the moon. Her voice was . . . well, the best word I can think of is *chalky*: dry, brittle, and easily cracked.

At one point I asked her, "What is depression like for you?"

Again the pause. "It's like when winter comes and the days get shorter and there's more and more darkness," she said. "But it's not just in the winter. It's all year, every day, like someone is slowly closing all the curtains of my house."

I asked her what she thought would happen to her. In the same flat, brittle tone, she said, "I think I'm dying."

As gently as I could, I asked, "Do you want to die?"

"Maybe it would be better," she said in a powdery whisper.

That was Paula "before."

Six weeks later we talked again. The change was dramatic. Paula held her head high. Her eyes shone. Her voice was fluid and clear, and her words came easily.

"How do you feel now?" I asked, although I could read the answer on her face.

"I feel," she said, "as if all the curtains have been drawn back. Now I am flooded with sunshine."

Paula was one of the people for whom Prozac happened to be the right choice at the right time. There are many other effective medications available for depression; it's possible one of them might have worked for her as well. Nevertheless, after a few weeks of treatment with Prozac, Paula broke free of her suffocating torment. Being in the supportive and stable environment of the hospital helped keep her life from spinning out of control. But clearly it was the use of medication that made the difference where it mattered most: *on the inside*.

In the previous chapters you've been given a look at depression and other psychiatric problems from the viewpoint of a doctor. The emphasis on the use of medications is understandable, given the fact that in our society people with medical degrees are the only ones legally able to prescribe drugs. (A book by a psychologist or a social worker would, of course, focus primarily on non-drug methods of treatment.) If the illness can be treated with medication, it would be a kind of malpractice—not to mention a form of cruelty—if the physician didn't at least offer patients the choice of trying something that has proved safe and effective for millions.

But how do things look from the perspective of the

people being treated? Before accepting a treatment recommendation, many patients ask some valid questions. What difference will a medication like Prozac make in their lives? What kind of reactions can they expect—not just from the medication, but from a society where psychiatric illness still carries an unfortunate stigma? What, in short, is life on Prozac like?

By way of answering, let me open my files and pull out reports on some of my patients. Afterward I'll give my responses to the questions people most often ask me about this important medication.

RHONDA'S STORY

At the age of forty-two, Rhonda had become the CEO of a New York public relations firm. It was a position she had earned after years of devoted work and after winning several industry awards. She was married to a producer for a TV network news organization whom she described as a "lovely and loving guy."

"If I'm riding so high," she wondered aloud during a visit to my office, "then why do feel I so low?"

Rhonda was depressed. She knew she wasn't reacting to the pressure of her new position because she had been battling her low mood for more than two years. She had been seeing a therapist since the problem began, but felt she was getting nowhere. Lately she was forcing herself to make the commute into work every morning. Once on the job she felt none of the enjoyment or excitement she thought would be there. She had trouble concentrating during meetings and was too tired to dream up new ideas for publicity campaigns. Most nights, after coming home, she fixed herself a huge plate of pasta and fell into bed, where she stayed until morning. She felt her condition was threatening not just her career but her marriage.

After examining her and talking with her at length, I suggested a stay in the hospital might offer a stabilizing environment that would help her get control of her life. I also suggested we try a course of treatment with Prozac.

Her brow, already knitted, became furrowed. "I've never used drugs before. I'm scared of them," she said. "I don't like the idea of using a chemical crutch." I explained how the medication could repair the biological problem that was causing her symptoms. She agreed to give it a try.

Rhonda made good progress during her hospital stay. While she didn't respond to the standard 20 mg dose, she did well at double that amount. She felt her energy and interest in life return to a level she hadn't known for years. After she left the hospital, she continued taking 40 mg of Prozac a day. The side effect she was most concerned about was drowsiness. "A sleepy exec is an ex-exec," she quipped. The medication did not sedate her, however, so this was no problem. If anything, her improved mood provided her with energy. Originally I had suggested that she take one capsule in the morning and one in the afternoon. She found she didn't like having to take a dose during working hours, so I agreed that she could take both capsules at breakfast.

When I last heard from her, Rhonda was back in control. Her job was bringing her the rewards she had hoped for, both material and otherwise. She had more energy to devote to her marriage. She reported feeling no side effects or other complications. As I write this, she has been off the medication for close to a year without experiencing recurring symptoms of her depression. "I have my fingers crossed," she said. "So do I," I said.

MICKI'S STORY

This twenty-seven-year-old woman worked as an editor at a magazine publishing company. Micki was by no means overweight, but for years she had struggled to keep to a low-calorie diet. She usually skipped breakfast and ate no more than a grapefruit or a small salad for lunch.

Soon, though, Micki began experiencing overwhelming food cravings late in the afternoon. She soon fell into the habit of bingeing on junk food and then making herself throw it all up. After some weeks she started bingeing and purging at lunch time and again a few hours later. Eventually the problem grew so bad that she was missing a lot of time at work, sometimes several days in a row. She saw a general practitioner and reported that she felt depressed, but was too ashamed to discuss her eating practices. The physician prescribed a tricyclic and told her to check back in a month or so.

When Micki found she had gained a few pounds, she stepped up her pattern of bingeing and purging. Her employer—herself a recovering bulimic—recognized what was happening and was sympathetic. She insisted that Micki get help. Micki talked to a nutritionist, who unfortunately misunderstood the nature of the problem. She assumed Micki was concerned about her weight because she worked in a magazine devoted to food and fashion. The nutritionist suggested some behavioral and dietary strategies. What she failed to realize, though, was that Micki's problem had a biological basis, possibly a serotonin defect, and that Micki needed medical treatment.

One night, after weeks of following her diet program, Micki went out of control. She went on a massive two-hour binge during which she also drank two bottles of wine. She passed out. Her roommate discovered her lying on her kitchen floor in a pool of vomit.

The next day she was admitted to the hospital. After she had been stabilized, I suggested we try an antidepressant. She didn't want a tricyclic, because she was worried about gaining weight. "No," I said, "I was thinking of Prozac," and I explained why.

A month later Micki felt strong enough to leave the hospital. She went back to her job. Naturally I stayed in touch with her. At last report she was still concerned about her weight but—with one notable exception during the Christmas holidays—had stopped bingeing completely. Her feelings of depression had vanished.

LUTHER'S STORY

With each passing day this thirty-seven-year-old computer programmer grew more and more concerned about dirt and germs in his environment. He bought rubber gloves by the gross and used them whenever he handled the newspaper or the telephone. Before opening a door he would whip out a handkerchief and wipe the knob, then would wipe his hand after he had closed the door behind him. He peeled the labels off canned goods so that he could wipe the cans free of "store dirt," as he called it. He was so fearful of contracting AIDS or cancer that he finally refused to visit friends or eat in restaurants. He took four showers a day (leaving work to do so), washed his hands almost constantly, and finally shaved his head because he feared his hair would become infested with "vermin."

Not surprisingly, Luther had trouble holding down a job. No environment was clean enough for him. He knew he was driving his family and friends crazy, but was powerless to stop himself. His wife bore the situation as long as she could, but finally brought him in for treatment. From the description of his symptoms and his behavior in the hospital—which he felt was a "hellhole of infection"—it was clear Luther had an obsessive-compulsive disorder.

I prescribed Prozac, 40 mg a day. Within five weeks his obsessions and compulsions had lessened. Five weeks more and they were all but gone. His behavior was under control and his mood improved. Once out of the hospital, Luther was able to find—and hold—a job. After a year of treatment, I asked whether he wanted to stop taking the medication. "Not yet," he said. I agreed to renew his prescription for another year. In my experience, I told him, there's a 50-50 chance he will need to keep taking the drug indefinitely. "That's okay," he replied. "A life on medication is better than no life at all."

KEVIN'S STORY

At thirty-two, this fit, active schoolteacher spent his summer months camping and hiking. His goal was to hike the entire length of the Appalachian Trail by the time he was thirty-five.

Last year, however, he returned from a camping expedition complaining of aching joints, especially in his ankles. The pain, which he attributed to a particularly difficult climb, was bad enough that he went to his family doctor, who gave him a complete physical but found nothing. "Take it easy on the mountains," was the doctor's advice.

Eventually the aches went away, but five months later they were back. Kevin also complained of low mood, irritability, and difficulty concentrating. He was absent from his teaching job for up to a week at a time. In his worst moments, he said, he wondered whether life was worth living if he could no longer teach or spend time outdoors.

An internist, sharp enough to ask if Kevin had spent time in the mountains, suspected Lyme disease—an arthritis-like condition spread through the bite of deer ticks. Sure enough, a blood sample confirmed the diagnosis. Kevin was given high doses of an antibiotic, which relieved his pain enormously.

His mood, however, continued to decline. The internist referred him to a neurologist who ordered a CAT scan. A close look at the image revealed a small lesion in Kevin's brain, a lingering result of the Lyme disease. At a social function, someone suggested that he ask his internist about Prozac. Kevin's doctor agreed that it was worth trying. Within a month, on 20 mg a day, Kevin's mood was back to normal. "This drug saved my life," he told me. "I guess I don't mean I would have slit my wrists, but it made it possible for me to keep enjoying the things that make my life worth living."

Paula, Rhonda, Micki, Luther, Kevin—five completely different stories, one happy ending. You'll note that, apart from responding well to Prozac, these people all have something in common. The medication didn't change their lives by making them smarter or stronger. They didn't take their pills, then wake up one morning, discover the cure for cancer, become president, end poverty and hunger, achieve world peace, and win the Nobel Prize in seven different categories. All Prozac basically did for them was *give them back their lives*— their normal, ordinary, very precious lives. Prozac doesn't work for everyone, and other drugs may work just as well. But it worked for these people, and it has worked for thousands more.

Let me now try to answer some of the basic questions you may have about this drug.

THE MOST COMMONLY ASKED QUESTIONS ABOUT PROZAC

"What will this medication do for me?"

One of the worst aspects of depression is the sense of utter hopelessness it inflicts on its victims. Depressed people see the future as holding nothing for them other than an unremitting and painful grayness. They are overwhelmed with guilt and shame and feel that they are completely helpless in the face of this relentless enemy. The glass is not just half empty; it's completely empty and the glass is shattered as well. Many severely depressed people find it almost impossible to move, let alone take a pill or talk to a therapist. No wonder so many contemplate—or actually commit—suicide.

One reason antidepressants often get such rave reviews from so many patients is this stark contrast between how bad the situation was before and how much better things seem after treatment has begun to work. For many people, relief of depression can make the difference between night and day. Many patients for whom Prozac is the answer make comments similar to Paula's: "It's like a veil lifting," said one. "Before, I felt like I was drowning," said another, "and now I've come up for air." I could fill an entire chapter with remarks like these.

Once depressed people begin to notice an improvement, no matter how slight, they often gain the strength they need to take the next step. Perhaps, then, the greatest gift an antidepressant medication can offer is hope—hope that the bad feelings will lessen, hope that life will once again be worth living.

"Is this drug a 'sure thing'?"

No medication works 100 percent of the time for 100 percent of the people who take it. On the average, for every ten people who take an antidepressant, perhaps seven can expect to feel some relief. If one drug doesn't work, we can try another that works differently.

People with depression tend to believe their situation is hopeless. In some cases, just getting them to accept treatment can be exhausting. If the first choice of therapy fails, not only must we start over, we may have to work even harder to convince the patient to keep trying. That's why good practice requires doctors to screen patients carefully so that they diagnose the problem accurately and improve their chances of choosing the right treatment from the outset. I try to caution the people in my care that we may not score our first time up, but try to hang on because we'll get another turn at bat.

"Does this drug cause side effects?"

Every person's body is different, and everyone will react differently to a medication. There is a good chance that any drug powerful enough to overcome an illness will produce at least some unwanted reactions. We just don't have the technology at this point to design medications that are specifically structured to attack only the precise cause of a given illness in a specific individual. Perhaps in the future patients will be able to insert their fingers in a machine that will diagnose their illness, analyze their DNA, mix some chemicals together, and dispense a tailor-made pill that doesn't cause side effects. That day, however, is a long way off.

I always try to alert my patients to the most common adverse reactions associated with a particular medication. My purpose is not to frighten them but to reassure them. When such side effects do occur, they are generally mild; people find they can put up with them for a while. They are certainly much less of a problem than the disease we're trying to conquer.

The most common problems I have seen in my practice are nausea, agitation, and trouble sleeping. Often these reactions go away within a week or two. One woman on Prozac told Fran Schumer, a writer from *New York* magazine, "If all my hair fell out, I'd still take it." Recently one of my own patients remarked, "Yes, my stomach felt a little queasy for a while, but my head felt so much better that it told my stomach to just deal with it."

Occasionally some of my patients on Prozac complain that they feel jittery or nervous and would rather switch to a different drug than take an additional medication that may be sedating. One patient told me his jaw hurt because he was constantly gritting his teeth. A woman interviewed in the same *New York* article described her time on Prozac as being "four months of crying every day." I have never seen that serious a reaction in my practice (and would have taken the patient off the drug much sooner than four months if I had), but I realize that Prozac is not the right choice for everyone.

"Will Prozac make me gain weight or lose sleep?"

Compared with the tricyclics, Prozac does not generally promote weight gain, although perhaps one in four people may notice an increase. Some people do lose weight while taking the drug; these tend to be people who were significantly overweight to begin with. Long-term studies show that the weight loss may stop after several months; continuing the drug after that point may not further reduce weight.

Insomnia may develop in perhaps 15 percent of people taking Prozac. In some cases it is severe enough that people stop the medication. In other cases people find they can tolerate the problem because it is outweighed by the improvement in their depression. As one patient said, "I'm having some trouble falling asleep, but I'm not sure if that's because of the medication or because I'm so excited about finally feeling the depression lift." Often, too, such side effects fade after a few weeks.

"Will I notice the benefit right away?"

Antidepressants are not like aspirin. It can take weeks for the benefits of Prozac and other products to show up, because the medication is changing the brain's basic neurochemistry. (Some people get better within a week, but generally these patients are probably experiencing a "placebo effect.") For some people, the long delay can be an ordeal; already feeling trapped by their oppressive illness, they are told they must wait perhaps a month before they see results. Imagine having to wait that long for your headache to go away! During this time I offer all the support I can as a physician, and may talk to others in the family to convey the importance of bearing with the patient while the medication takes effect. The old cliché sometimes applies to treatment for depression: The darkest hour is just before the dawn.

"How long will I have to take the medication?"

When some people learn that their depression arises from a chemical imbalance, they are concerned that they will have to take antidepressants for the rest of their lives. In some cases that may be true. Usually, however, I ask patients to keep using the medication for six months to a year after their symptoms disappear. If the problem recurs after they stop the medication, I ask them to get in touch with me to discuss whether they should start taking the drug again.

Prozac makes such a difference in some people's lives that they want to go on using it indefinitely. Asked by the *New York* reporter if she thought she'd have to take Prozac forever, one woman replied, "I hope so." One of my patients wondered if I could write her enough prescriptions in advance so that she could lay in a ten-year's supply in case the drug was withdrawn from the market. (I told her no.)

"Is there a chance I'll get hooked on this drug?"

Recently I recommended Prozac for one of my patients, whose name was Lynnette. She said, "Is that the one everyone thinks is so great they want to keep taking it forever? No thanks. I don't want to turn into a drug addict." I explained that antidepressants are not usually addicting, although some people may become psychologically dependent on them. A few who respond to the medication understandably feel that without it they may sink back into the pit of depression. In most cases, however, once antidepressants have corrected the physical problem that produces the symptoms, people can stop using the medication. If symptoms return, another round of medication may be needed, but ideally the goal of therapy is to live normally again without the need for continuous treatment. In Lynnette's case, she agreed to try Prozac. Her depression lifted and she had no trouble stopping the medication a year later.

"Will I experience withdrawal when I stop taking Prozac?"

Not likely. The body takes a long time to break down Prozac. Four or more weeks may elapse before the last traces of the medication are eliminated. Stopping the drug usually will not lead to any abrupt reactions. "When I was taking the drug," one patient reported, "I felt like I was being gently lifted up out of a deep pit. After I stopped using it, I felt like I kept moving forward because of my own momentum."

"Will Prozac make me high?"

Antidepressants including Prozac don't get you stoned or give you a buzz. People who have been trapped by depression do find the return to normality elating. "I'm back to normal," one patient told me not long ago. "For me, that's the true wonder of these 'wonder drugs.' " Some people on Prozac do report feeling a caffeine-like reaction. If this becomes a serious problem they might switch to another medication. Prozac does not usually produce any effect at all in people who are not suffering from some form of depression.

"Will Prozac affect my sex life?"

The people I treat with Prozac report very few sexually related problems that can be definitely traced to the medication. It's much more often the case that people whose depression has lifted can once again enjoy life's pleasures—not just sex, but food and friendship as well. "It's like my senses have been in the shop for repair," remarked one woman, "and now they're back and working again." Of course, people who are no longer depressed are much easier to be around. They are no longer weighed down by feelings of hopelessness and fatigue; their thoughts are no longer bleak. Obviously, such people will be more energetic and attractive. With depression out of the way, all aspects of life improve. Relationships become more stable. Couples argue less and enjoy each other more, in bed as well as out of it.

Reports indicate that perhaps 2 percent of people taking Prozac may notice a change in their level of sexual interest. Less than 1 percent of men report abnormal ejaculation or impotence, while women may report a delay or loss of orgasm. One of my patients on Prozac did remark that, while his depression had lifted, he didn't seem as interested in sex as he had been before the illness struck, a change he attributed to the medication. I asked if he wanted me to take him off the drug. He thought for a moment and said, "No. Feeling good twenty-four hours a day is probably better than feeling good twenty minutes twice a week."

In another case a woman reported that her depression had lifted, but she no longer seemed to be able to reach orgasm. I offered to switch medications, but she decided to stick with the Prozac. Within two months her orgasms returned to normal. A recent report suggests that ejaculation problems in men taking Prozac may respond to treatment with an antihistamine called Periactin.

"I might become pregnant. Should I take Prozac?"

I never prescribe any medication for pregnant women. If a woman expecting a baby demands some kind of drug treatment, I will refer her to another physician. I also strictly warn women of child-bearing age that they should not get pregnant while taking any antidepressant. If they do they must discontinue the drug. As a rule, such medications have not been shown to damage the fetus, but I see no point in taking any chances. Interestingly, the bodily changes during pregnancy can sometimes protect women against depression; women known to be depressed often feel better and exhibit fewer symptoms while they are expecting. Once these women have delivered their child, however, I watch them very carefully and usually treat their depression aggressively.

We don't know if Prozac passes into breast milk, but many drugs do, so I advise new mothers who need antidepressants to plan on bottle-feeding their infants. Ordinarily, of course, breast-feeding would be preferable, but I believe treating the depression takes priority. A mother who is relieved of her illness is better able to bond with her child and tend to the child's needs.

"Is Prozac safe for older patients?"

One person I treated was a seventy-two-year-old woman named Martha, who told me she had been depressed since she'd turned sixty. Previous drug treatments hadn't helped her, but she agreed to give Prozac a try. Generally, because their bodies are changing and are more sensitive to side effects, older people respond to lower doses of medication. In this case, my patient did very well on 10 mg of Prozac a day—half the usual dosage. Two months after treatment began, Martha came to see me. "I'm so tickled," she said. "I went to a meeting last week and everyone wanted to know what was different about me. I didn't tell them, and they all decided I must have had plastic surgery because I looked ten years younger."

We're not always so lucky, however. Another of my patients, a seventy-five-year-old man, had previously tried a series of tricyclics and MAOI's. He had even undergone a dozen electroconvulsive treatments, which produced only temporary results. Prozac made no significant difference either. He never did get better; he simply went home from the hospital and returned to his old routine. He agreed with me that we couldn't really blame the drug. In his case, his depression was of a type that just couldn't be reached by any of the treatments currently available. Had he been younger, perhaps medications or even ECT might have made a difference, but there's no way of knowing for certain.

"Should a child or a teenager take Prozac?"

Recognizing depression in younger people can be tricky. Their bodies are changing quickly, and they are very sensitive to the emotional pressures of growing up. It's sometimes hard to know which of their problems result from clinical depression and which arise from the usual "rites of passage." Nonetheless, some young people are clearly clinically depressed, and there is evidence suggesting the rate of depression in this age group is on the rise. The risk is higher among those whose parents also suffer from some form of psychiatric disorder. While cognitive or behavioral therapy may be very effective for depressed young people, antidepressants, including Prozac, can sometimes be a useful addition in severe cases. Any child taking such medications should be closely supervised by an experienced physician.

"What will people think if they find out I take medication for a psychiatric illness?"

If they're smart, they'll commend you for getting the help you need, just as they would if you underwent surgery for cancer or took nitroglycerine tablets for your heart. It's true that many people (including some doctors) don't understand that depression, eating disorders, obsessive-compulsive disorder, and other related problems are often biological illnesses that respond to biological treatment.

I see signs that our society is changing, that "confessions" about their problems by celebrities and other talk-show guests are contributing to a new openness. Misunderstandings are still inevitable. But if some insensitive or uninformed people react negatively when they learn you are in treatment, you have three basic choices: ignore them, avoid them, or try to educate them. Loaning them this book is a good way to start.

"Didn't I hear on the news that Prozac makes people suicidal?"

I find this question extremely frustrating. I am concerned that people are being misinformed and are thus misled into worrying about a problem that doesn't really exist. But I need a whole chapter to respond fully. Read on.

CONTROVERSY:
CAN PROZAC KILL?

Within two years after being introduced on the market, in January 1988, Prozac was a roaring success. Hundreds of thousands of people had been lifted from their depression. What's more, the medication was being used to relieve crippling anxiety, obsessive behavior, and a host of other conditions. Not only did most of the 1.5 million people using Prozac get better, they didn't experience some of the annoying side effects that had made previous treatment hard to bear. Prozac was by no means a cure-all or a perfect drug. Not everyone noticed improvement, and some stopped taking it because of nausea, agitation, insomnia, or other problems. For many people, however, the medication meant the difference between night and day.

In mid-September 1989, newspapers reported that an out-of-work printer from Louisville, Kentucky, had gone on a shooting rampage in the print shop where he had once been employed. He killed eight people and wounded a dozen others before turning the gun on himself. An autopsy revealed that he had been taking Prozac.

Then some researchers at Harvard Medical School, Martin Teicher, M.D., Carol Glod, R.N., and Jonathan O. Cole, M.D., published a report in the February 1990 issue of the *American Journal of Psychiatry* claiming that "six depressed patients free of recent serious suicidal ideation developed intense, violent suicidal preoccupation after two to seven weeks of fluoxetine treatment." In this report, the authors describe patients with various illnesses, including depression, who reported the onset of suicidal thoughts and behavior. The paper raised the question of whether these developments were the direct result of treatment with Prozac.

As I'll explain in detail in a moment, there were many problems with this report. It was at times self-contradictory, which severely undermined the validity of its conclusions. And as a scientist with years of experience in clinical research, I found it virtually impossible to interpret. Nonetheless it was enough to help trigger what can only be called media backlash. Suddenly Prozac was back in the headlines again, and the news was not good.

Soon afterward more people began claiming that Prozac caused people to become violent or to experience suicidal feelings. One woman appeared on a talk show to denounce the product and announce that she was forming the National Prozac Survivors Support Group. Soon chapters had sprung up in five states from California to Florida. Members demanded that the drug be recalled.

In July the Cable News Network asked its viewers to call a 900 number and vote on which stories they wanted to see covered on the next morning's newscast. The Prozac controversy was one of the top two vote-getters among 1400 callers, so the story appeared the following day.

In August the *New York Times* ran a prominent article

in its Health section summarizing the Harvard report and the ensuing legal turmoil surrounding Prozac. The story was syndicated nationwide. The principal author of the report, Dr. Teicher, even appeared on television to discuss the findings.

Phones began ringing in medical offices across the country. Patients, scared out of their wits, were calling to know if they should toss their Prozac capsules into the trash. I received many such calls myself. In one typical instance, I heard from a woman who had been under my care but who had since moved to another state. She said that because of the media coverage her current doctor had taken her off Prozac, which had relieved her depression, and switched her to a tricyclic. Now she could tell that she was beginning to relapse. "What can I do?" she asked, a nervous edge to her voice. "I'm so scared of being sick again." I told her I had read the Harvard report carefully and saw no reason to worry. Far greater than the risk of suicidal thoughts, I said, was the risk that people like herself who stopped taking their medication might suffer needlessly.

By the end of summer 1990, Prozac's manufacturer was facing a flurry of lawsuits. Some of these suits were filed by the survivors of victims from the print-shop massacre, including the family of the gunman. Other suits were launched by individuals, including a salesman from the Chicago area who claimed he deliberately tried to smash his car into a truck while on Prozac. A Canadian man filed a claim stating that he developed tremors two weeks after taking the medication. A Long Island woman charged that Prozac plunged her into a eighteen-month-long suicidal rage during which she tried to kill herself 150 times with everything from scissors and shower hooks to screws pulled from a hospital chair.

The suits demanded payments for damages ranging from over $1 million to $150 million. Generally the suits charged that the Eli Lilly company failed to inform doctors about a link between Prozac and suicidal or violent behavior. They also charged that the drug was unsafe and had not been adequately tested before release. The suit by the founder of the support group sought unspecified damages and accused Lilly of negligence, breach of warranty, and fraud. Some of the suits also named the patients' doctors as sharing in the liability. As supporting evidence, these suits often cited the Harvard paper.

Lilly hasn't publicly commented on the suits except to state that Prozac is safe. Nevertheless, in May of 1990 Lilly added "suicide attempt" to the list of precautions about possible adverse reactions. This list appears as part of the official prescribing information that is distributed with each bottle of Prozac and that appears with every advertisement for the product in professional journals. Some physicians, concerned about their patients (and about malpractice suits), stopped prescribing the drug altogether.

The flames were fanned again in November 1990 when a man indicted for assassinating Meir Kahane, founder of the Jewish Defense League, was found to have been taking Prozac, along with "three or four" other psychiatric medications.

WHAT'S GOING ON?

Elsewhere in this book I have stated my position: that Prozac can be a good choice of treatment for many people with certain clearly identifiable psychiatric illnesses. I have reviewed the safety data and, as I hope I have communicated in previous chapters, have found little cause for alarm. On the contrary: I find cause for reassurance. Some of that reassurance comes from the data on over 11,000 patients who took the drug in clinical trials. These data showed that suicidal ideation may follow the start of antidepressant treatment in a small minority of patients, but that the incidence is higher among patients taking tricyclic antidepressants or even a placebo than it is with Prozac.

Historically, of course, there are several instances where problems with medications have emerged only after a drug has appeared on the market. In some cases these drugs have been withdrawn, so there is good reason for people to be concerned about reports of potential dangers. Apart from the clinical data, then, my other source of reassurance comes from my own first-hand experience. Like the researchers who wrote the Harvard report, my practice is based in a hospital that primarily treats the most severely ill patients. Not once have I seen a problem arise involving suicidal thoughts or violent behavior that could be linked to the use of Prozac. An informal survey among my colleagues and a review of hospital records has also failed to turn up any signs of trouble.

Why all the fuss then? Does Prozac triggers suicidal ideation? The only scientifically reasonable answer is: perhaps—in rare cases. Physicians must watch for signs of suicidality in *all* their depressed patients, not just those on Prozac. It is not possible to say such a problem will never arise. If it does, we can withdraw the drug. In the meantime the best we can do is study the data and continue to use any medication cautiously and judiciously.

But is the Harvard report that raised the issue really valid? When measured by established scientific standards, the answer seems to be no.

CLOSE-UP: THE SUICIDE REPORT

The weaknesses of the Harvard report fall into five main categories.

Problem #1: Defining "Suicidal Preoccupation"

One main problem with the Harvard report is that it implies there are different types and degrees of suicidality. The authors observe that their patients were "free of recent *serious* suicidal ideation" (emphasis added). They explain later that all of these individuals had had suicidal thoughts in the past, but that these weren't considered to be serious because they were passive in nature—"I wish I were dead"—and were thus nothing to be concerned about.

Nowhere in the medical literature, however, is a distinction made between "serious" and "unserious" suicidal thoughts. Nor is there a clinical difference between passive and active thoughts. *Both* types of thoughts can lead to a suicidal act. I would argue that *any* suicidal ideation is a matter of utmost seriousness and must be attended to. Thus, the researchers begin their report by defining suicidality in ways that are not generally recognized among the medical profession.

Another major problem is that the authors did not use a standardized scale to assess the severity of suicidal impulses in an objective way. The researchers appear to rely instead on their own subjective assessments, which makes it impossible for others to judge the degree of "serious" suicidality and thus to confirm the findings for themselves.

The researchers state in the summary that, before taking Prozac, their patients had been free of *recent* suicidal thoughts. If that's all you read of the report, you might even come away with the impression that these people never had suicidal thoughts at all

Delving into the details of the cases, however, you'd get a different picture entirely. For example, the authors state that "Ms. A" had a seventeen-year history of depression, among the symptoms of which were "occasional passive suicidal thoughts." "Mr. B" and "Ms. C" both had passive suicidal thoughts a mere *two weeks* before starting Prozac; Ms. C even had "a history of mild suicidal gestures." During the preceding eight years "Ms. D" had become enraged and had made at least three serious suicide attempts by taking drug overdoses.

Two years before taking Prozac, "Ms. E" had reported having persistent suicidal thoughts. "Ms. F" had made "three significant suicide gestures" in the past thirteen years, and for the past five years had experienced "intermittent suicidal thoughts."

Thus, strangely, the researchers apparently define "recent" to mean occurring only within the last two weeks. The authors claim that their patients' histories of suicidal feelings were irrelevant because those feelings were judged as "passive." Yet some of the patients had acted on their feelings by making suicidal gestures. What's more, the researchers acknowledge that in some cases the patients made "serious" or "significant" suicide attempts, but imply that because these events took place two or five or thirteen years ago they are not recent and so they don't really count.

I believe the compelling evidence showing that the six patients in this report had suicidal tendencies before they began taking Prozac is enough to undermine the credibility of the findings.

Problem #2: Factual Errors

In their introduction, the Harvard researchers state that "standard antidepressants are not known to induce severe and persistent suicidal ideation in depressed patients" who had been free of such thoughts before undergoing treatment. This isn't true. There are numerous reports in the literature dating back more than twenty years of suicidal thoughts that were associated with the use of standard antidepressants, especially the tricyclics. Amitriptyline, the most widely prescribed antidepressant in the world, has been associated in some patients with suicidal threats and paranoid thoughts. Both amitriptyline and imipramine are associated with aggressive or assaultive behavior. Another report found that suicidal feelings emerging in patients taking desipramine vanished when they were switched to Prozac.

As an article in *International Drug Therapy Newsletter* points out, however, these other studies "cast doubt on a causal connection between suicidality and the antidepressant therapy. They also document that some patients who become suicidal during treatment with one therapy may be treated with fluoxetine without the emergence of suicidal ideation and [still experience] a complete remission of depression."

The Harvard report is trying to suggest that antidepressant therapy, in this case with Prozac, led to suicidality. Yet the authors themselves remind the reader that by relieving depression, medications can energize patients. People who could barely walk before may feel well enough to get back into the swing of things again. Thus their energy may return, *but the suicidal feelings they experience as a symptom of their illness may persist.* Although the drug is working, patients may still feel like killing themselves, and now they've regained the strength to do it. That's why all patients in this stage of treatment need to be watched very closely. That's also why it's extremely difficult to prove that suicidal feelings are "caused" by a drug, when we know that such feelings are often caused by the illness itself. Paradoxically, successful drug therapy can lead some patients to act on their self-destructive impulses.

At the end of their report, the authors state that all of these patients had been "hopeful and optimistic" before taking Prozac. That's very odd, considering that hopefulness and optimism are the very *antithesis* of depression. Indeed, I can't think of any depressed patient I've treated who displayed anything *but* hopelessness to one degree or another. Such a remark on the part of the researchers calls into question either their diagnosis or their interpretation of the term *hopeful.*

Problem #3: Procedural Errors

No standard patient profile: The writers conclude that "in our experience, this side effect [suicidality] has

occurred in 3.5 percent of patients receiving fluoxetine.
. . . They go on to note that, statistically speaking, such
a finding means that perhaps as many as eight out of
one hundred patients on Prozac are at high risk of
suicide. Yet nowhere in their report do they provide the
data to substantiate this astounding claim. Who are
these patients? How were they chosen? Were they rep-
resentative of all patients under treatment at the time, or
were they among the very sickest? Were they drawn from
among all patients at the hospital, or just those seen by
one particular doctor? We are not told. I'm not the only
one who noticed this glaring omission; a letter to the
editor published in the same journal in November 1990
also pointed it out. As Dr. Richard A. Miller put it: "The
conclusion . . . is simply not supported by [the] case
presentations."

Too few cases: Another procedural problem is the
small number of patients included in this report. Case
reports are the weakest form of science, and six cases
are not usually enough to establish a true trend. Researchers who draw conclusions based on half a dozen
cases usually strive to select only the "purest" examples,
cases that are not complicated by other severe illnesses
or forms of treatment. Such is not the case here, as I'll
explain further below.

In science, there is safety in numbers: The bigger
your study, the more secure you can be in your findings.
That's why statistical analysis is so important. If you only
study two patients, and one develops Side Effect X, you
can't validly make the claim that "50 percent of all people
taking this drug will experience Side Effect X." In a
group of one hundred patients, it might turn out that,
still, only that one person noticed that side effect—a rate
of only 1 percent. Again, close analysis of data will reveal
whether this was a true medical finding or whether it
was merely a coincidence. Drs. Maurizio Fava and Jerrold
Rosenbaum, another team of researchers, became concerned about the potential impact of the Harvard report

and did their own analysis of the data. In a presentation before the American Psychiatric Association's annual meeting in November 1990, they reported that the incidence of suicidality associated with Prozac was not significantly different than the rate seen with other medications.

Conclusion comes before the facts: Because the authors of the Harvard report do not state how they gathered their data, we can only speculate about their method of research. From what we are given, however, it appears that one day the authors noticed a patient on Prozac was experiencing suicidal thoughts. Instead of posing a hypothesis—"Does Prozac cause a greater risk of suicidal ideation than other antidepressants?"—and designing an experiment to answer that question, the authors seem to have looked back over their case files to find other examples. In other words, they appear to have worked backward from the ideal scientific approach: They suspected Prozac was responsible for suicidality, and then looked for other cases to back up this foregone conclusion. Such retrospective analysis, if handled very cautiously, can sometimes generate valid (albeit tentative) conclusions, but it is the weakest form of science because the researchers' bias can creep in and undermine the validity of the findings.

Equally serious is the fact that the investigators were fully aware of what drugs the patients were receiving. In scientific terms, they were not "blind." Blindness—for purposes of research, anyway—is essential. Let me explain.

Think of the statues of Justice you've seen in every movie that has scenes set in a courthouse. Justice wears a blindfold and holds a pair of scales. Perhaps a similar statue should be placed in every research lab in the country, since scientists should also weigh all of their evidence without bias or prejudice.

The Harvard report was not blind. The researchers knew their patients were taking fluoxetine, and thus they could have been biased when they went back over the records looking for other cases. In the best kind of scientific study, the researchers would establish the hypothesis first: "Does fluoxetine cause suicidality?" They would give patients either the drug or placebo in blind fashion, then sit back and observe.

Problem #4: Control Errors

The Harvard report was also flawed because it was not controlled. In research, "control" means you make sure that all conditions *except one* are exactly the same in all groups under study. If the research is not well controlled, you'll never be completely sure which effects are the result of which factors.

This can be explained with a simple example. Suppose your Aunt Fanny and your Aunt Margaret wanted you to judge whose chocolate cake was better. It wouldn't be a fair trial if you tasted one cake after starving yourself for three days and the other cake after eating a seven-course meal. Obviously your response will be affected by your degree of appetite and the sensitivity of your taste buds. Better to control the experiment by tasting both cakes under identical conditions. That way the only factor you've changed is the cake being tasted.

The Harvard researchers did not set things up to rule out the impact of other factors. One factor they should have screened for is the effects of multiple medications.

One patient in the report, for example, had been taking an antidepressant and two antianxiety drugs, but stopped a month before beginning treatment with Prozac. The other five patients in their report were taking at least one other drug along with Prozac at some point in their treatment. Mr. B, Ms. C, and Ms. E had all been given an MAOI two weeks before Prozac; Ms. C was also taking an antipsychotic along with Prozac and Ms. B had lithium plus Prozac for a period of two weeks. Ms. D started with Prozac; two weeks later she reported suicidal feelings and also developed a severe rash, for which she was given an antihistamine and a steroid. Ms. F was the most complicated of all: She was taking one drug to reduce mania, one for hypertension, a thyroid medication, a diuretic, and Valium. And Prozac was added on top of this chemical cocktail!

The patients were also given different doses of Prozac, ranging from 20 mg to 80 mg per day. Although some people do need higher doses, many depressed patients respond to 20 mg a day or less. Because the dosage wasn't controlled, it's not possible to know whether higher doses put people at higher risk of suicidal feelings.

The only sure way to know that a drug is responsible for an effect is to compare results between patients given a placebo and those given the active medication. A valid study would be one comparing emergence of suicidality in depressed people treated with Prozac and in depressed people given a placebo, but that's not what we're dealing with here.

Another problem was that the researchers didn't control for diagnosis. In other words, with the possible exception of Mr. B (who had been depressed for twenty-one years), these people were not just depressed, they also had a vast range of very severe illnesses. Ms. A was an alcohol abuser; Ms. C had paranoia, bulimia, and agoraphobia; Ms. D was a recovering alcoholic with borderline personality disorder; Ms. E had borderline personality disorder and a form of epilepsy; Ms. F, whose brain waves appeared abnormal on an EEG reading, also had a history of bipolar disorder, multiple personality disorder, and hypothyroidism. These were severely ill individuals with some severe medical problems. With such complicated problems, it is just not possible to reach the simplistic conclusion that "Prozac causes suicidality."

One other point: As mentioned earlier, antidepressants such as the tricyclics can be fatal in overdose, and some people (around forty for every million prescriptions) use these medications as their suicide weapon. As several dozen reports on overdose have suggested, however, it seems to be very difficult to kill yourself by taking large doses of Prozac. The fact that antidepressants have been associated with suicide in the past has led researchers to come up with newer and safer drugs, which was part of the reason Prozac was invented in the first place.

Problem #5: Side Effect Patterns

Usually the side effects associated with a particular medication come and go in a certain pattern. In other words, if ten patients out of a hundred are going to experience nausea, for example, then most of those patients will notice the nausea at about the same time, and the nausea will disappear about the same time once the drug is stopped.

The Harvard case reports show wide fluctuations in the type, onset, severity, and abatement of side effects related to Prozac. Suicidality—the side effect in question here—took anywhere from eleven days to seven weeks to show up. Even more strangely, it took anywhere from three days to three months to disappear. Earlier I explained that Prozac takes about a month to clear from the body. Yet Ms. A, who had been taking Prozac for eleven days, reported that suicidality abated after three days. Mr. B took Prozac for a month (along with lithium for two of those weeks), yet reported suicidal thoughts that persisted for two months after the last traces of the Prozac should have been eliminated. During those two months he was also given two tricyclics and an MAOI.

As a scientist, I am inclined to interpret such findings to mean that the suicidal thoughts were probably *not* caused by the medication. To say that Prozac was the "cause" of suicidality in such cases is like saying, "These patients all ate breakfast; therefore, breakfast triggers suicidal feelings."

The case reports also indicate that three of the patients had what appeared to be toxic or adverse reactions to Prozac. Ms. C experienced restlessness, and Ms. D and Ms. F developed a severe rash. Normally, these would be signs that the patient was possibly allergic to the drug, and that it should be withdrawn immediately. If a doctor notices these complications and does not stop the drug, it is usually for one of two reasons. Either the doctor feels the drug is working on the main problem and that the benefits outweigh the risks, or there is no other option left to help the patient. In these cases, two of these patients were given even *higher* doses of Prozac—from 20 mg to 40 mg a day in the first case, and from 60 to 80 mg a day in the second. Apparently the physicians felt the drug was helping, since they raised the dosage instead of stopping the medication when trouble arose. Yet in none of the six cases did depression appear to improve after Prozac was started.

Since half of these patients appeared to have toxic or other adverse reactions, and since none experienced relief of depression, it's possible that these individuals were simply among the 30 percent of depressed people who are not candidates for treatment with Prozac in the first place. That is a far cry, however, from concluding that the drug is unsafe or that it causes suicidal feelings.

If we can conclude anything from the Harvard report, the most we can say is that "six people with long histories of lots of different life-threatening psychiatric problems and histories of suicidality who were taking lots of different drugs experienced suicidal feelings at the time they were taking Prozac or Prozac plus at least one other medication." The vast majority of people taking Prozac today obviously do not fit into this very extreme category.

THE MEDIA CIRCUS

Let's consider why the Harvard report received such an enormous amount of attention in the media.

Perhaps the problem goes back a couple of years to the day the drug was originally launched into the market. The manufacturer believed it had a good and worthy product on its hands. Like any business, the company knew it needed to make a profit. Prozac was promoted vigorously to the people who would ultimately be responsible for its success: the doctors. Reports of safety and efficacy were played up in the lay press as well. The upshot of all this was that expectations surrounding Prozac were extraordinarily high from the beginning. Perhaps some of these expectations were unrealistic. Prozac may have been inadvertently set up early on as a target for later criticism.

As has been well demonstrated during recent political campaigns, television is hardly the ideal medium for thoughtful, deep analysis of complicated issues. Even the best news people cannot possibly convey, in a two-minute report filled with ten-second sound bites, all the implications of complex scientific data that have been gathered over months or even years. Broadcasters hired for their looks, not their educational backgrounds, aren't qualified to spot the defects in scientific studies and explain them clearly to their audiences. Newspapers and magazines are perhaps a little better at providing thoroughness and balance, but even there space is limited. Deep analysis is usually the provenance of books like this one. But books take months to prepare, while newspapers appear overnight and TV appears instantly. Once those first impressions are formed in the public's mind, they are very hard to expunge.

It may appear that I am criticizing the Harvard report unfairly. Perhaps the authors intended nothing more than to raise a warning flag, to alert us to a potential danger. Doing so is a valid function of medical literature, and many patients (not to mention their physicians) have benefited from information distributed in this way. After all, Lyme disease first came to our awareness as a series of anecdotal reports from a few puzzled physicians in the

Northeast. Certainly, if a medication can drive patients to suicide, we all want to know about it.

The accepted practice for physicians with such preliminary information is to report it in the form of letters to the editor. In this case, however, the report appeared as a full-blown article in a highly respected professional journal. The title of the article was "Emergence of Intense Suicidal Preoccupation During Fluoxetine Treatment." Such a title is somewhat misleading, because it does nothing to indicate that the report is merely a series of patient anecdotes and not a formal scientific study.

Normally this would not be a very serious issue. The problem in this case is that the media spotted the article and immediately leaped to some unfounded conclusions. For example, Chris Wallace and other reporters appeared on ABC Television's "Nightline" program to discuss this "major study." As we have seen, the Harvard report was neither major nor a study. Writing in *The Harvard Mental Health Newsletter*, Maurizio Fava, M.D., and Jerrold F. Rosenbaum observe that the findings, "uncritically reported in the mass media, must be put into perspective." They go on to state that "In a survey of 1000 cases treated with antidepressants, including 300 treated with fluoxetine alone, we found none resembling those in the recent highly publicized report—even though doctors have prescribed fluoxetine more often to suicidal patients because the chance of death from an overdose is so low."

THE BOTTOM LINE

The next time you hear a medical report on the news, whether it's about Prozac or any other discovery, keep your skeptical antennae raised. If going to a medical library and reading the original report for yourself is out of the question, do the next best thing: Assess what you're being told by asking three vital questions:

How many patients were in the study? The more there are, the greater the chance that the reports are valid. The lawsuits against Lilly—citing the Harvard report on six patients—charge that Prozac was not fully tested before release and is unsafe. Yet before Prozac was approved in this country, almost 11,000 people took part in clinical trials. The record of safety and effectiveness was strong in Europe, where fluoxetine had been used for some time, and further research done here was convincing enough that the FDA approved the product for release. Over a million more people have used the drug in the past two years, and its record of safety and efficacy continues to be impressive.

Were the researchers "blind"? Did they know what medications the patients were on, or did they observe the results without being biased? Even better, was the study "double-blind"—that is, were both patients and caregivers unaware of who was taking the drug and who was getting the placebo? Was the study prospective (planned in advance) or retrospective (done after the fact)? Also, did the study design involve a "cross-over"? In other words, did the researchers give the patients the medication for a while and then switch them to a placebo to see if there was any difference? If so, our confidence in the findings is even stronger.

Was the study well controlled? Did the investigators make sure the patients were as alike as possible, especially in type and severity of illness, and that only one factor was changed—the drug, the dosage, or other forms of therapy?

If all of these conditions have been met chances are good that the findings are valid. The Harvard report met none of these criteria. Nonetheless the media, naive about science and always eager to report the bad news about the good news, blew its findings out of proportion.

How the lawsuits will be resolved, we don't yet know. We do know that the future availability of an effective medicine may be in serious jeopardy.

BEYOND DEPRESSION:
THE FUTURE OF PSYCHIATRY

Prozac is the first of a new generation of medicines, the serotonin uptake blockers. By zeroing in on one defective neurotransmitter system and ignoring the others, Prozac apparently helps repair the damage without disrupting other bodily functions—the chemical equivalent of a surgical strike.

But there's still room for improvement. New drugs are coming down the pipeline that may offer even greater efficacy with even better safety. Some of these medications are nothing more than a gleam in a research scientist's eyes; others have been used for years in other countries; still others are now making their way through the tortuous federal approval process and may even be available by the time you read this book.

What, then, does the future hold? What developments can we expect to see in our understanding of depression and other psychiatric illnesses? Will we one day have available a pill that will cure depression, crippling anxiety, substance abuse? How will our approach to treatment change based on these discoveries?

OTHER DRUGS

Even as you read this, a scientist somewhere is sitting in front of a computer watching the brightly colored image of a molecule form on the screen. By punching buttons and entering data, this scientist is trying to figure out which chemicals—even ones that have never been seen before—can bond to this molecule and what will happen when they do. Eventually this scientist will print out the data and hand it to some chemists, who will then assemble their test tubes and pipettes and set to work creating the chemical based on the computer's design specs. After this chemical has been tested inside and out, the next "miracle drug" will be born.

That event is years away, however. The drug most likely to arrive next is another serotonin uptake inhibitor whose generic name is sertraline, now under development by the Roerig division of Pfizer Pharmaceuticals. The manufacturer applied for FDA approval in mid-1988. (It takes an average of two and a half years for the FDA to reach a decision.) Preliminary evidence suggests that in addition to being an antidepressant, sertraline helps reduce appetite and may be approved for treatment of obesity. Until studies have been published and we've been able to use this drug on a lot of patients, we can't be sure what advantages this drug may offer over Prozac or other drugs.

Fluvoxamine, a chemical cousin of fluoxetine (the active ingredient in Prozac), was introduced as Faverin in the United Kingdom in 1986. Manufactured by Reid-Rowell, it may be available for use in this country in a few years. It, too, works directly on the serotonin system and, like Prozac, reduces the symptoms seen in obsessive-compulsive disorder. One recent study found fluvoxamine to be about as effective for OCD as Prozac and clomipramine, which is the only drug currently approved for use in this disorder. Fluvoxamine can cause gastrointestinal side effects and agitation, but most OCD patients seemed to be able to tolerate the drug.

In addition to the serotonin blockers, new antidepressants in other categories are also on the horizon. For example, L-deprenyl (also known as selegiline) is related to the MAO inhibitors. Early reports suggest it relieves depression and poses less risk of causing high blood pressure, which is a problem commonly seen with other drugs in this group.

Mianserin is now used for depression and anxiety in Europe and the United Kingdom. This drug appears to affect the serotonin system as well as the histamine system. Some studies find mianserin to be about as good as Prozac in reducing depression; one report, however, found it wasn't significantly better than a placebo. Researchers have also reported that patients using Prozac experienced a greater reduction in suicidal feelings than on mianserin, even though their depression was equally severe, and that mianserin caused weight gain while Prozac induced weight loss. One study suggests that mianserin may be good for patients who need combination therapy with an MAOI and another drug, since mianserin doesn't interact with MAOI's the way Prozac and other antidepressants can.

Oxaprotiline is a relative of maprotiline (which is sold under the name Ludiomil). Both of these drugs are members of the class known as tetracyclic antidepressants (tetracyclic means "four rings," compared to the three-ring tricyclic antidepressants). While still in the early stages of development, some studies suggest oxaprotiline is an effective antidepressant with minimal side effects.

To make their marks, new drugs have to hold some advantage over existing therapies; otherwise there's no compelling reason to invent (or use) them. Paroxetine (which will be made by SmithKline Beecham under the name Aropax or Seroxat) may hold an edge over Prozac because it leaves the body more quickly. Approval for paroxetine was applied for in November 1989, so it may not appear on the market until 1992 or so.

Lab studies show that citalopram, a drug in use in Denmark, may be more selective for the serotonin system than either Prozac or paroxetine, which may translate into a better side-effects profile. Hoffmann–La Roche recently released moclobemide, an MAOI that is more selective (and thus safer) than its predecessors and that may eliminate the dietary restrictions associated with use of other drugs in this group.

S-adenosyl-methionine (known by the chummy acronym SAM) is different from any other kind of antidepressant. SAM occurs naturally in the human body. Studies in Europe and Great Britain suggest that SAM, given intravenously, can improve depression rapidly. If so, that would be a big improvement over the standard antidepressants, which can take weeks to kick in.

Future drugs will no doubt be targeted to affect specific neurotransmitter systems. We know that the serotonin system involves at least six different receptors. That knowledge may lead to drugs that even target specific *sub*systems—working on Receptors 1, 3, and 5, for example, but leaving 2, 4, and 6 alone. In fact, Bristol-Myers is developing gepirone, which appears to target just one serotonin subsystem. Another neurotransmitter system is called gamma-aminobutyric acid (GABA) and is part of a different group entirely than the monoamines (the group to which serotonin belongs). Ciba-Geigy is working on a drug (so far known only by the homely name CGP-35348) that blocks one of two receptors in the GABA system.

In addition to discovering new drugs, we may find additional uses for established drugs. For example, alprazolam, an antianxiety agent related to Valium, seems to work as well as the standard tricyclic antidepressant amitriptyline in cases of mild depression (though not for severe depression). Buspirone, another antianxiety drug, may work against depression when given in higher doses.

Another strategy involves creating new dosage forms for existing drugs to help patients with special needs. Apparently the makers of Prozac are working on a liquid form of the drug to make it easier to take for patients who can't swallow capsules or who can get by with less than the standard 20-mg dose.

The possibilities, it appears, are endless.

DIAGNOSTIC TESTS

Doctors today use a variety of blood tests, urine tests, hormonal assays, and other strategies to peek into the body and see what's going on there. More and more psychiatrists are (or should be) turning to the medical lab for help with the diagnosis and treatment of their patients. In the near future we may have tests that reveal specific conditions and indicate which patients may be good candidates for which antidepressants.

For example, when serotonin is broken down by enzymes, the pieces of the serotonin molecules are flushed out in the urine. Some fascinating research is showing that people who have abnormally low levels of serotonin by-products are much more susceptible to such problems as violent behavior. When we have enough data, we may one day be able to screen patients for this sign that something is wrong with their neurochemistry, and perhaps treat them with medications to prevent disaster from striking. Similar tests may be found to identify people with certain subtypes of obsessive-compulsive disorder, eating disorders, and so on.

Imagine undergoing a complete physical and being handed a report listing not only your blood type but your "neurotransmitter profile" as well. That's not too far-fetched.

THE GROWTH OF BIOPSYCHIATRY

When doctors confront a new or poorly understood disease, their tendency is to assume that the problem arises from the complex interplay of many factors: biological, psychological, social. Participants in the very first international conference on AIDS, for example, believed that the disease arose from a range of causes. Now we know that AIDS is caused by a virus.

The same general shift from the complex to the simple has occurred throughout the history of psychiatry. At one time we thought phobias were the result of misplaced sexual impulses. Now we know that they have their root in a physical problem in the brain. Autism used to be attributed to bad parenting. Now we have evidence that it, too, is the result of a serotonin defect. Recently researchers using advanced imaging technology found that hyperactivity and schizophrenia result from lesions in certain parts of the brain.

This growing awareness of the biological basis of mental disorders led to the growth of biopsychiatry. As a biopsychiatrist myself, I believe that ultimately we will be able to trace virtually all psychiatric illnesses back to their source: the brain. If this model is valid—and the evidence is mounting that it is—then the chances are high that medicines will offer the greatest hope for relief. If your symptoms arise from a leak in your neurological plumbing, years of psychotherapy won't do you as much good as a round of medication. Medical treatment, in the hands of people who are trained to administer it, is often the safest, fastest, most effective, and least expensive approach. That's a pretty hard combination to beat.

That's not to say that other forms of psychotherapy don't have their place. It's possible that therapy can help people to reprogram themselves to learn new kinds of healthier behavior or ways of thinking. Until recently, psychotherapy had not been subjected to the same rigorous scientific testing that medicines must undergo.

Only now do we have at hand some clear-cut studies showing which methods are best. We are also gathering a great deal of evidence showing that behavioral changes resulting from psychotherapy actually lead to chemical and structural changes in brain tissue, just as medications do. But I believe that if a medication can "cut to the chase" and produce those same desirable changes quickly and safely, then the drug should be used. I see no need to make my patients walk eastward all around the world when all they really need to do is walk one block to the west.

A FINAL WORD

Depression is a devilish disease because, like the Devil, it lies. It wraps the brain in a black blanket and robs its victims of health, of happiness, of hope.

But there *is* hope. If you suffer from depression or another disorder that has drained your life of color and joy, *you can get better*. It will take effort, even though you think you haven't the strength to go on. It may take time, even if you think your time may be running out. It may take the help of other people, whether they are doctors, family members, or friends.

In his book *Darkness Visible*, William Styron reports that his battle with depression nearly drove him to suicide. Yet he got treatment, and because of it he survived to write, not a suicide note, but a moving account of both the tragedy of this illness and the joy that accompanies its lifting. "Depression is not the soul's annihilation," he observes. "It is conquerable."

Whether victory comes as a result of medication, counseling, or even the comforting word of a loving voice, it will be a victory nonetheless, a prize beyond price.

BIBLIOGRAPHY

Altamura, A. C., S. A. Montgomery, J. F. Wernicke. "The Evidence for 20 mg a Day of Fluoxetine as the Optimal Dose in the Treatment of Depression." *British Journal of Psychiatry*, 1988; 153(suppl. 3):109–112.

American Psychiatric Association. *Diagnostic and Statistical Manual of Mental Disorders* (third edition—revised). Washington: American Psychiatric Press, 1987.

Angel, Itzchak, Marie-Anne Taranger, Yves Claustre, *et al.* "Anorectic Activities of Serotonin Uptake Inhibitors: Correlation with Their Binding *In Vitro*." *Life Sciences*, 1988; 43(8):651–658.

Angier, Natalie. "Eli Lilly Facing Million-Dollar Suits on Its Antidepressant Drug Prozac." *The New York Times*, August 16, 1990, p. B13.

Aranow, Robert B., James I. Hudson, Harrison G. Pope, Jr., *et al.* "Elevated Antidepressant Plasma Levels After Addition of Fluoxetine." *American Journal of Psychiatry*, July 1989; 146(7):911–913.

Baldessarini, Ross J., Elda Marsh. "Fluoxetine and Side Effects" [letter]. *Archives of General Psychiatry*, February 1990; 47:191–192.

Beck, Aaron T., A. John Rush, Brian F. Shaw, Gary Emery. *Cognitive Therapy of Depression*. New York: The Guilford Press, 1979.

Beck, Melinda, Geoffrey Cowley. "Beyond Lobotomies." *Newsweek*, March 26, 1990.

Bell, Iris R., Jonathan O. Cole. "Fluoxetine Induces Elevation of Desipramine Level and Exacorbation of Geriatric Nonpsychotic Depression" [letter]. *Journal of Clinical Psychopharmacology*, December 1988; 8(6):447–448.

Bergstrom, R. F., L. Lemberger, N. A. Farid, R. L. Wolen. "Clinical Pharmacology and Pharmacokinetics of Fluoxetine: A Review." *British Journal of Psychiatry*, 1988; 153(suppl. 3):47–50.

Bianchi, Michael D. "Fluoxetine Treatment of Exhibitionism" [letter]. *American Journal of Psychiatry*, August 1990; 147(8):1089.

Bluestone, Mimi, Alfred Pedersen. "Fighting Depression with One of the Brain's Own Drugs." *Business Week*, February 22, 1988, pp. 156, 158.

Bodkin, J. Alexander, Martin H. Teicher. "Fluoxetine May Antagonize the Anxiolytic Action of Buspirone." *Journal of Clinical Psychopharmacology*, April 1989; 9(2):150.

Bouchard, Roch H., Emmanuelle Pourcher, Pierre Vincent. "Fluoxetine and Extrapyramidal Side Effects" [letter]. *American Journal of Psychiatry*, October 1989; 146(10):1352–1353.

Bower, B. "Antidepressant Helps Obsessive-Compulsives." *Science News*, May 21, 1988; 133:324.

Bowsher, Dennis J., Howard Rowe, Nagy A. Farid, *et al.* "Pressor Responses to Tyramine and Norepinephrine After Subchronic Administration of Fluoxetine to Man." *Life Sciences*, 1988; 42(25):2569–2575.

Breed, Allen G. "Anti-depressant Pill Called Big Risk. Ex-Users Form Self-help Groups, Say Drug Promotes Violence and Suicide." *The Sacramento Bee*, June 7, 1990, p. A12.

Brod, Thomas M. "Fluoxetine and Extrapyramidal Side Effects" [letter]. *American Journal of Psychiatry*, October 1989; 146(10):1353.

Browning, W. Nicholson. "Exacerbation of Symptoms of Multiple Sclerosis in a Patient Taking Fluoxetine" [letter]. *American Journal of Psychiatry*, August 1990; 147(8):1089.

Burket, Roger C., John D. Hodgin. "Fluoxetine Treatment of a Depressed Patient Susceptible to Malignant Hyperthermia" [letter]. *American Journal of Psychiatry*, May 1989; 146(5):680.

Byerley, William F., Fred W. Reimherr, David R. Wood, Bernard I. Grosser. "Fluoxetine, a Selective Serotonin Uptake Inhibitor, for the Treatment of Outpatients with Major Depression." *Journal of Clinical Psychopharmacology*, 1988; 8(2):112–115.

Cammer, Leonard. *Up from Depression*. New York: Pocket Books, 1971.

Carfagno, Jacalyn, Doug Carroll. "Eli Lilly Falls 3⅞ on News of Lawsuit." *USA Today*, July 19, 1990, p. 3B.

"The Chemistry of Despair." *The Economist*, June 16, 1990, pp. 95–96.

Cohen, Bennet J., Michael Mahelsky, Lenard Alder. "More Cases of SIADH with Fluoxetine." *American Journal of Psychiatry*, July 1990; 147(7):948–949.

Cole, William. "New Drugs for Depression." *Better Homes and Gardens*, April 1988, p. 73.

Cooper, Glenn L. "The Safety of Fluoxetine—An Update." *British Journal of Psychiatry*, 1988; 153(suppl. 3):77–86.

Cooper, Steven J., Colin T. Dourish, David J. Barber. "Fluoxetine Reduces Food Intake by a Cholecystokinin-Independent Mechanism." *Pharmacology Biochemistry & Behavior*, 1990; 35(1):51–54.

Cowen, R. "Sociopaths, Suicide and Serotonin." *Science News*, October 14, 1989; 136:250.

Cowen, Ron. "Receptor Encounters: Untangling the Threads of the Serotonin System." *Science News*, October 14, 1989; 136:248–250, 252.

Cowley, Geoffrey. "The Promise of Prozac." *Newsweek*, March 23, 1990, pp. 38–41.

Cunningham, Malcolm, Kip Cunningham, R. Bruce Lydiard. "Eye Tics and Subjective Hearing Impairment During Fluoxetine Therapy." *American Journal of Psychiatry*, July 1990; 147(7):947–948.

Damluji, Namir F., James M. Ferguson. "Paradoxical Worsening of Depressive Symptomatology Caused by Antidepressants." *Journal of Clinical Psychopharmacology*, 1988; 8(5):347–349.

Dasgupta, Krishna, Cynthia E. Hoover, Richard A. Miller, Richard B. Berkley. "Additional Cases of Suicidal Ideation Associated with Fluoxetine" [letters, plus reply from Martin H. Teicher *et al.*]. *American Journal of Psychiatry*, November 1990; 140(11):1570–1572.

Extein, Irl, Peter L. Herridge, Larry S. Kirstein. *New Medicines of the Mind.* New York: Borkley Books, 1990.

Falk, William B. "Suit: Drug Prompted Suicide Attempts." *Newsday*, July 18, 1990, p. 8.

Fava, Maurizio, Jerrold F. Rosenbaum. "Does Fluoxetine Increase the Risk of Suicide?" *The Harvard Mental Health Letter*, January 1991; 7(7):8.

Fava, Maurizio, Jerrold F. Rosenbaum. "Suicidality and Fluoxetine: Is There a Relationship?" in New Research Program and Abstracts. 143rd Annual Meeting of the American Psychiatric Association. Washington, D.C.: APA, 1990.

Fawcett, Jan, John M. Zajecka, Howard M. Kravitz, *et al.* "Fluoxetine versus Amitriptyline in Adult Outpatients with Major Depression." *Current Therapeutic Research;* May 1989; 45(5):821–832.

Ferguson, James M. "Treatment of an Anorexia Nervosa Patient with Fluoxetine" [letter]. *American Journal of Psychiatry*, September 1987; 144(9):1239.

Ferguson, James M., John P. Feighner. "Fluoxetine-Induced Weight Loss in Overweight Non-Depressed Patients." *International Journal of Obesity*, 1987; 11(suppl. 3):163–170.

Forrest, David V. "Reappearance of Menses in a Patient Taking Fluoxetine" [letter]. *American Journal of Psychiatry*, February 1990; 147(2):257.

Franklin, Erica. "Treating Anxiety Like the Blues." *American Health*, March 1990, p. 46.

Gelenberg, Alan J. "The Perils of Prozac." *Biological Therapies in Psychiatry Newsletter*, November 1990; 13(11):1–2.

Gelman, David. "Drugs vs. the Couch." *Newsweek*, March 26, 1990, pp. 42–43.

Giesecke, Mark E. "Overcoming Hypersensitivity to Fluoxetine in a Patient with Panic Disorder" [letter]. *American Journal of Psychiatry*, April 1990; 147(4):532–533.

Goff, Donald C., Andrew W. Brotman, Meredith Waites, Scott McCormick. "Trial of Fluoxetine Added to Neuroleptics for Treatment-Resistant Schizophrenic Patients." *American Journal of Psychiatry*, April 1990; 147(4):492–494.

Gold, Mark S., Michael Boyette. *Wonder Drugs: How They Work.* New York: Pocket Books, 1987.

Goldman, Marcus J., Lester Grinspoon, Susan Hunter-Jones. "Ritualistic Use of Fluoxetine by a Former Substance Abuser." *American Journal of Psychiatry*, October 1990; 147(10):1377.

Goleman, Daniel. "Depressed Parents Put Children at a Greater Risk of Depression." *The New York Times*, March 30, 1989, p. B17.

Goode, Erica E. "Beating Depression." *U.S. News & World Report*, March 5, 1990, pp. 48–51, 53, 55–56.

Goode, Erica. "Secret Obsessions." *Vogue*, February 1989, pp. 246, 248–249.

Goodnick, Paul J. "Influence of Fluoxetine on Plasma Levels of Desipramine" [letter]. *American Journal of Psychiatry*, April 1989; 147(4):552.

Gorman, Jack M., Michael R. Liebowitz, Abby J. Fyer, *et al.* "An Open Trial of Fluoxetine in the Treatment of Panic Attacks." *Journal of Clinical Psychopharmacology*, October 1987; 7(5):329–332.

Gould, Mark A. *A Consumer's Guide to Psychiatric Diagnosis.* Summit, New Jersey: The PIA Press, 1989.

Graham, Peter M., Kenneth F. Ilett. "Danger of MAOI Therapy After Fluoxetine Withdrawal" [letter]. *The Lancet*, November 26, 1988; 1255–1256.

Hadley, Ann, M. Pat Cason. "Mania Resulting from Lithium-Fluoxetine Combination" [letter]. *American Journal of Psychiatry*, December 1989; 146(12):1637–1638.

Hall, John: "Fluoxetine: Efficacy Against Placebo and by Dose—An Overview." *British Journal of Psychiatry*, 1988; 153(suppl. 3):59–63.

Halper, James P., J. John Mann. "Cardiovascular Effects of Depression Medications." *British Journal of Psychiatry*, 1988; 153(suppl. 3):87–98.

Hansen, Thomas E., Kay Dieter, George A. Keepers. "Interaction of Fluoxetine and Pentazocine" [letter]. *American Journal of Psychiatry*, July 1990; 147(7):949–950.

Hedges, Chris. "F.B.I. Investigates Group of Zealots Who Praise Kahane Slaying." *The New York Times*, November 13, 1990, pp. B1, B4.

Hindmarch, Ian. "A Pharmacological Profile of Fluoxetine and Other Antidepressants on Aspects of Skilled Performance and Car Handling Ability." *British Journal of Psychiatry*, 1988; 153(suppl. 3):99–104.

Hollander, Eric, Michael R. Liebowitz, Ronald Winchel, *et al.* "Treatment of Body-Dysmorphic Disorder with Serotonin Reuptake Blockers." *American Journal of Psychiatry*, June 1989; 146:768–770.

Hon, David, Sheldon H. Preskorn. "Mania During Fluoxetine Treatment for Recurrent Depression." *American Journal of Psychiatry*, December 1989; 146(12):1638–1639.

Humphries, John E., Munsey S. Wheby, Scott R. Van den Berg. "Fluoxetine and the Bleeding Time." *Archives of Pathology and Laboratory Medicine*. July 1990; 114:727–728.

Hwang, Andrew S., Richard M. Magraw. "Syndrome of Inappropriate Secretion of Antidiuretic Hormone Due to Fluoxetine" [letter]. *American Journal of Psychiatry*, March 1989; 146(3):399.

"In Defense of Fluoxetine." *International Drug Therapy Newsletter*, October 1990; 25(8):1–2.

Jenike, Michael A., Lynn Buttolph; Lee Baer, *et al.* "Open Trial of Fluoxetine in Obsessive-Compulsive Disorder." *American Journal of Psychiatry*, July 1989; 146(7): 909–911.

Jonas, Jeffrey M., Mark S. Gold, L. Bunte, A. L. C. Pottash. "Weight Loss Effect of Fluoxetine in Normal-Weight and Overweight Bulimics" [abstract]. Paper presented at 1988 Annual Meeting of the Society for Neuroscience, Toronto, Canada, November 13–18.

Kalliel, John N. "Aquagenic pruritus." *Journal of the American Academy of Dermatology*, June 1989; 20(6):1123.

Kessler, David A., Wayne L. Pines. "The Federal Regulation of Prescription Drug Advertising and Promotion." *JAMA*, November 14, 1990; 264(18):2409–2415.

Klein, Donald F. "Repeated Observations of Yawning, Clitoral Engorgement, and Orgasm Associated with Fluoxetine Administration" [letter, plus response from Modell]. *Jour-*

nal of Clinical Psychopharmacology, October 1989; 9(5):384.

Klerman, Gerald L. "The Current Age of Youthful Melancholia: Evidence for Increase in Depression Among Adolescents and Young Adults." *British Journal of Psychiatry*, 1988; 152:4–14.

Klerman, Gerald L., Myrna M. Weissman. "The Interpersonal Approach to Understanding Depression." In: Theodore Millon, Gerald L. Klerman, eds. *Contemporary Directions in Psychopathology*. New York: The Guilford Press, 1986.

Kline, Mark D. "Fluoxetine and Anorgasmia" [letter]. *American Journal of Psychiatry*, June 1989; 146(6):804–805.

Kovacs, Maria. "Psychotherapies for Depression." In: Lester Grinspoon, ed. *Psychiatry Review Update* (vol. 2, part 5). Washington: American Psychiatric Press, 1983.

Laakmann G., D. Blaschke, R. Engel, A. Schwarz. "Fluoxetine vs Amitriptyline in the Treatment of Depressed Outpatients." *British Journal of Psychiatry*, 1988; 153(suppl. 3):64–68.

Lader, Malcolm. "Fluoxetine Efficacy vs Comparative Drugs: An Overview." *British Journal of Psychiatry*, 1988; 153(suppl. 3):51–58.

Lebegue, Breck. "Mania Precipitated by Fluoxetine" [letter]. *American Journal of Psychiatry*, December 1987; 144(12):1620.

Lemberger, Louis, Howard Row, Janet C. Bosomworth, *et al.* "The Effect of Fluoxetine on the Pharmacokinetics and Psychomotor Responses of Diazepam." *Clinical Pharmacology and Therapeutics*, 1988; 43:412–419.

"Let's Talk Facts About Manic-Depressive Disorder." Washington, D.C.: American Psychiatric Association, 1988.

Levine, Louise R., Sidney Rosenblatt, Janet Bosomworth. "Use of the Serotonin Re-Uptake Inhibitor, Fluoxetine, in the Treatment of Obesity." *International Journal of Obesity*, 1987; 11(suppl. 3):185–190.

Levine, Robert, Joel S. Hoffman, Eileen Day Knepple, Michael Kenin. "Long-term Fluoxetine Treatment of a Large Number of Obsessive-Compulsive Patients." *Journal of Clinical Psychopharmacology*, August 1989; 9(5):281–283.

Levine, S., R. Deo, K. Mahadevan. "A Comparative Trial of a

New Antidepressant, Fluoxetine." *British Journal of Psychiatry*, 1987; 150:653–655.

Liebowitz, Michael R., Eric Hollander, Janet Fairbanks, Raphael Campeas. "Fluoxetine for Adolescents with Obsessive-Compulsive Disorder." *American Journal of Psychiatry*, March 1990; 147(3):370–371.

Liebowitz, Michael R., Eric Hollander, Frank Schneier, *et al.* "Fluoxetine Treatment of Obsessive-Compulsive Disorder: An Open Clinical Trial." *Journal of Clinical Psychopharmacology*, 1989; 9(6):423–427.

"Lilly Stock Plunges on Drug Data." *Chicago Tribune*, October 20, 1990, p. C3.

Linet, Leslie S. "Treatment of a Refractory Depression with a Combination of Fluoxetine and d-amphetamine." *American Journal of Psychiatry*, 1989; 146(6):803–804.

Lopez-Ibor, Juan J., Jr. "The Involvement of Serotonin in Psychiatric Disorders and Behaviour." *British Journal of Psychiatry*, 1988; 153(suppl. 3).26–39.

Lund, Diane S. "Cognitive-behavioral Therapy Found Helpful for Depressed Teenagers." *The Psychiatry Times*, June 1990, p. 46.

March, John S., Hugh Johnston, John H. Griest. "Obsessive-Compulsive Disorder." *American Family Physician*, May 1989; 39(5):175–182.

Marcus, Marsha D., Rena R. Wing, Linda Ewing, *et al.* "A Double-Blind, Placebo-Controlled Trial of Fluoxetine Plus Behavior Modification in the Treatment of Obese Binge-Eaters and Non-Binge-Eaters." *American Journal of Psychiatry*, July 1990; 147(7):876–881.

Markovitz, Paul J., Susan J. Stagno, Joseph R. Calabrese. "Buspirone Augmentation of Fluoxetine in Obsessive-Compulsive Disorder." *American Journal of Psychiatry*, June 1990; 147(6):798–800.

Martensson, B., S. Nyberg, G. Toresson, *et al.* "Fluoxetine Treatment of Depression." *Acta Psychiatrica Scandinavia* 1989; 79:586–596.

Milam, James R., Katherine Ketcham. *Under the Influence: A Guide to the Myths and Realities of Alcoholism.* New York: Bantam Books, 1983.

Miller, Lucinda G., Robert C. Bowman, Debra Mann, Ashok Tripathy. "A Case of Fluoxetine-Induced Serum Sickness." *American Journal of Psychiatry*, December 1989; 146(12):1616–1617.

Mintzer, Mary: "Crossing the Border." *Health*, December 1987, p. 16.

Modell, Jack G. "Repeated Observations of Yawning, Clitoral Engorgement, and Orgasm Associated With Fluoxetine Administration" [letter]. *Journal of Clinical Psychopharmacology*, February 1989; 9(1):63–65.

Montgomery, S. A., H. Dufour, S. Brion, *et al.* "The Prophylactic Efficacy of Fluoxetine in Unipolar Depression." *British Journal of Psychiatry*, 1988; 153(suppl. 3):69–76.

Montgomery, Stuart A. "The Benefits and Risks of 5-HT Uptake Inhibitors in Depression." *British Journal of Psychiatry*, 1988; 153(suppl. 3):7–10.

Moore, Jeffrey L., Robert Rodriguez. "Toxicity of Fluoxetine in Overdose" [letter]. *American Journal of Psychiatry*, August 1990; 147(8):1089.

Muijen M., D. Roy, T. Silverstone, *et al.* "A Comparative Clinical Trial of Fluoxetine, Mianserin, and Placebo in Depressed Outpatients." *Acta Psychiatrica Scandinavia*, 1988; 78:384–390.

Musher, Jeremy S. "Anorgasmia with the Use of Fluoxetine" [letter]. *American Journal of Psychiatry*, July 1990; 147(7):948.

Nakra, Bharat R. S., Peggy Szwabo, George T. Grossberg. "Mania Induced by Fluoxetine" [letter]. *American Journal of Psychiatry*, November 1989; 146(11):1515–1516.

Naranjo, Claudio A., Karen E. Kadlec, Pablo Sanhueza, *et al.* "Fluoxetine Differentially Alters Alcohol Intake and Other Consummatory Behaviors in Problem Drinkers." *Clinical Pharmacology and Therapeutics*, 1990; 47: 490–498.

National news column [CNN audience votes for Prozac story]. *Star-Tribune*, Minneapolis–St. Paul, July 25, 1990, p. 7A.

Nicholson, A. N., Peta A. Pascoe. "Studies on the Modulation of the Sleep-Wakefulness Continuum in Man by Fluoxetine, a 5-HT Uptake Inhibitor." *Neuropharmacology*, 1988; 27(6):597–602.

Papolos, Demitri F., Janice Papolos. *Overcoming Depression*. New York: Harper & Row, 1987.

Papp, Laszlo A., Jack M. Gorman. "Suicidal Preoccupation

During Fluoxetine Treatment" [letter, plus response from Martin Teicher]. *American Journal of Psychiatry*, October 1990; 147(10):1380–1381.

Pappas, Nancy. "Skinny Pills." *Woman's Day*, June 20, 1989, p. 37.

Pary, Raymond, Carmelita Tobias, Steven Lippmann. "Fluoxetine: Prescribing Guidelines for the Newest Antidepressant." *Southern Medical Journal*, August 1989; 82(8).1005–1009.

Pigott, Teresa A., Michele T. Pato, Suzanne E. Bernstein, *et al.* "Controlled Comparisons of Clomipramine and Fluoxetine in the Treatment of Obsessive-Compulsive Disorder." *Archives of General Psychiatry*, October 1990; 47:926–932.

Pohland, Raymond C., Tonik K. Byrd, Marta Hamilton, John R. Koons. "Placental Transfer and Fetal Distribution of Fluoxetine in the Rat." *Toxicology and Applied Pharmacology*, 1989; 98:198–205.

"Police Say Kahane Suspect Took Anti-Depressant Drugs." *The New York Times*, November 9, 1990, p. B3.

Pope, Harrison G. Jr., James I. Hudson. *New Hope for Binge Eaters*. New York: Harper & Row, 1984.

Pope, Harrison G., Susan L. McEloy, Paul E. Keck, Jr., James I. Hudson. "Long-term Pharmacotherapy of Bulimia Nervosa" [letter]. *Journal of Clinical Psychopharmacology*, October 1989; 9(5):385–386.

Pope, Harrison G., Jr., Susan L. McElroy, Ralph A. Nixon. "Possible Synergism Between Fluoxetine and Lithium in Refractory Depression." *American Journal of Psychiatry*, October 1988; 145(10):1292–1294.

Preskorn, Sheldon H., Jorge H. Beber, John C. Faul, Robert M. A. Hirschfeld. "Serious Adverse Effects of Combining Fluoxetine and Tricyclic Antidepressants" [letter]. *American Journal of Psychiatry*, April 1990; 147(4):532.

Ramirez, Luis C., Julio Rosenstock, Suzanne Strowig, Susan Cercone, Philip Raskin. "Effective Treatment of Bulimia with Fluoxetine, a Serotonin Uptake Inhibitor, in a Patient with Type I Diabetes Mellitus." *The American Journal of Medicine*, May 1990; 88:540–541.

Regush, Nicholas. " 'Wonder Drug' Target of Suits; Side Effects Are Alleged for Anti-Depression Pill. *Montreal Gazette*, August 21, 1990, p. A3.

Riddle, Mark A., Nancy Brown, David Dzubinski, *et al.* "Fluoxetine Overdose in an Adolescent." *Journal of the American Academy of Child and Adolescent Psychiatry*, 1989; 28(4):587–588.

Riddle, Mark A., James F. Leckman, Maureen T. Hardin, *et al.* "Fluoxetine Treatment of Obsessions and Compulsions in Patients with Tourette's Syndrome." *American Journal of Psychiatry*, September 1988; 145(9):1173–1174.

Riggs, Joy. "Lawsuit Targets Lilly Drug." *The Indianapolis News*, August 8, 1990, p. C10.

Rudorfer, Matthew V., Potter, William Z.: "Combined Fluoxetine and Tricyclic Antidepressants" [letter, plus reply from Dr. Vaughan]. *American Journal of Psychiatry*, April 1989; 147(4):562–563.

Salama, Azia A., Moustafa Shafey. "A Case of Severe Lithium Toxicity Induced by Combined Fluoxetine and Lithium Carbonate" [letter]. *American Journal of Psychiatry*, February 1989; 146(2):278.

Schenker, Steven, Richard F. Bergstrom, Robert L. Wolen, Louis Lemberger. "Fluoxetine Disposition and Elimination in Cirrhosis." *Clinical Pharmacology and Therpeutics*, 1988; 44:353–359.

Schmidt, Michale J., Ray W. Fuller, David T. Wong. "Fluoxetine, a Highly Selective Serotonin Reuptake Inhibitor: A Review of Preclinical Studies." *British Journal of Psychiatry*, 1988; 153(suppl. 3):40–46.

Schraml, Frank, Gary Benedetti, Kenneth Hoyle, Anita Clayton. "Fluoxetine and Nortriptyline Combination Therapy." *American Journal of Psychiatry*, December 1989; 146(12):1636–1637.

Schumer, Fran. "Bye-Bye, Blues: A New Wonder Drug for Depression." *New York*, December 18, 1989, pp. 48–53.

Sholomskas, Alan J. "Mania in a Panic Disorder Patient Treated with Fluoxetine" [letter]. *American Journal of Psychiatry*, August 1990; 147(8):1090–1091.

Sobin, Paul, Lon Schneider, Helen McDermott. "Fluoxetine in the Treatment of Agitated Dementia" [letter]. *American Journal of Psychiatry*, December 1989; 146(12): 1636.

Sternbach, Harvey. "Danger of MAOI Therapy After Fluoxetine

Withdrawal" [letter]. *The Lancet*, October 8, 1988: 850–851.

Styron, William. *Darkness Visible: A Memoir of Madness*. New York: Random House, 1990.

Swerdlow, Neal R., Ana Maria Andia. "Trazodone-Fluoxetine Combination for Treatment of Obsessive-Compulsive Disorder" [letter]. *American Journal of Psychiatry*, December 1989; 146(12):1637.

"Tailoring Treatment for Depression's Many Forms." *U.S. News & World Report*, March 5, 1990, pp. 54–55.

Teicher, Martin H., Carol Glod, Jonathan O. Cole. "Emergence of Intense Suicidal Preoccupation During Fluoxetine Treatment." *American Journal of Psychiatry*, February 1990; 147(2):207–210.

Teuting, Patricia, Stephen H. Koslow, Robert M. A. Hirschfeld. *Special Report on Depression Research*. National Institute of Mental Health Science Reports. Rockville, Maryland: National Institute of Mental Health, 1981.

Vaughan, D. A. "Interaction of Fluoxetine with Tricyclic Antidepressants" [letter]. *American Journal of Psychiatry*, November 1988; 145(11):1478.

Wilcox, James Allen. "Abuse of Fluoxetine by a Patient with Anorexia Nervosa" [letter]. *American Journal of Psychiatry*, August 1987; 144(8):1100.

Wong, David T., Leroy R. Reid, Penny G. Threlkeld. "Suppression of Food Intake in Rats by Fluoxetine: Comparison of Enantiomers and Effects of Serotonin Antagonists." *Pharmacology Biochemistry & Behavior*, 1988; 31(2):475–479.

Young, J. P. R.; A. Coleman, M. H. Lader: A Controlled Comparison of Fluoxetine and Amitriptyline in Depressed Outpatients." *British Journal of Psychiatry*, 1987; 151:337–340.

INDEX

Jeffrey M. Jonas, M.D., is Director of Clinical Research and Director of Alcohol Treatment at Fair Oaks Hospital in Summit, New Jersey. A graduate of Amherst College, he earned his medical degree from Harvard, where he also completed his postgraduate medical training. He served as Medical Director of the clinical research unit at Harvard's McLean Hospital and was a member of the Medical School faculty. At Fair Oaks Hospital, he established the Eating Disorders Program, which is now known throughout the country for its innovative approach to treatment. Dr. Jonas is the author of over sixty professional articles and publications discussing his clinical research in such areas as psychopharmacology, eating disorders, and affective disorders.

Ron Schaumburg is a medical writer specializing in psychiatric subjects. He has ghostwritten books on a range of topics including sleep disorders, eating disorders, cults, illicit drugs, addiction, and depression. He edits material for a psychiatric newsletter and has written educational pamphlets for both professionals and lay readers on a number of medications including Prozac. He is a member of the American Medical Writers Association.